Finding Your Path, Engaging Your Purpose

How to Engage the Power of Intention To Discover and Fulfill Your Destiny

Blythe Ayne, PhD

Finding Your Path, Engaging Your Purpose

How to Engage the Power of Intention To Discover and Fulfill Your Destiny

Blythe Ayne, PhD

Finding Your Path, Engaging Your Purpose

How to Engage the Power of Intention to Discover and Fulfill Your Destiny

Blythe Ayne, PhD

LARGE PRINT

Emerson & Tilman, Publishers
129 Pendleton Way #55
Washougal, WA 98671

All Rights Reserved
No part of this publication may be reproduced, distributed, or transmitted in any form, or by any means, including photocopying, recording, or other electronic or mechanical methods, without the prior written permission of the author, except brief quotations in critical reviews and other noncommercial uses permitted by copyright law.

All written materials and graphics – Copyright © Blythe Ayne
Photos – With Sincere Gratitude to:
Lars Nissen, FietzFotos, Lolame and Pixabay

www.BlytheAyne.com
Blythe@BlytheAyne.com

Finding Your Path, Engaging Your Purpose
Excellent Life Series – Book 4

ebook ISBN: 978-1-947151-96-3
Paperback ISBN: 978-1-947151-97-0
Large Print ISBN: 978-1-947151-98-7
Hardbound ISBN: 978-1-947151-99-4
Audio book ISBN: 978-1-957272-07-8

[BODY, MIND & SPIRIT / Inspiration & Personal Growth
BODY, MIND & SPIRIT / Mindfulness & Meditation
BODY, MIND & SPIRIT / Healing/Prayer & Spiritual]

DEDICATION

"A path is made by walking on it."
Chuang Tzu

This book is dedicated to those who now set foot
Upon their unique path.

Books & Audiobooks by Blythe Ayne, Ph.D.

Nonfiction:

How to Save Your Life Series:
Save Your Life with the Dynamic Duo – D3 and K2
Save Your Life With the Phenomenal Lemon & Lime
Save Your Life With the Power Of pH Balance
Save Your Life with Stupendous Spices
Save Your Life with the Elixir of Water

Excellent Life Series:
Love is the Answer
45 Ways to Excellent Life
Life Flows on the River of Love
Finding Your Path, Engaging Your Purpose
Horn of Plenty — The Cornucopia of Your Life

Absolute Beginner Series:
Bed Yoga–Easy, Healing, Yoga Moves You Can Do in Bed
Bed Yoga for Couples–Easy, Healing, Yoga Moves You Can Do in Bed
Write Your Book! Publish Your Book! Market Your Book!

Fiction:

Adult Mystery–The Joy Forest Mystery Series
A Loveliness of Ladybugs
A Haras of Horses
A Clowder of Cats
A Gaggle of Geese

YA Science Fiction–The Darling Undesirables Series
The Heart of Leo - short story prequel
The Darling Undesirables
Moons Rising
The Inventor's Clone
Heart's Quest

Short Story Collections & Novellas:
6 Minute Stories
13 Lovely Frights for Lonely Nights
When Fields Hum and Glow

Children's Illustrated Books:
The Rat Who Didn't Like Rats
The Rat Who Didn't Like Christmas

Poetry, Photography & Art:
Home & the Surrounding Territory

Audiobooks:
Save Your Life With the Phenomenal Lemon & Lime
Save Your Life with Stupendous Spices
The Darling Undesirables
The Heart of Leo

Blythe Ayne's paperback, large print, hardback books, ebooks & audiobooks
are found wherever books are sold.
www.BlytheAyne.com

Table of Contents

1. Expand Your Reality Transform Your Circumstances	1
2. Imagination, Creativity, & Genius	25
3. Clarify Your Intention & Cast Out Your Doubts	31
4. The Future is NOW! Learn to Think from the End	43
5. Believing & Behaving "As If" Embracing Abundance	57
6. You Are a Part of Everything How to Attract What You Desire	87
7. Release What Others Expect of You & Do No Be Aggrieved	107
8. Have Respect for Yourself Lay Claim to Personal Strength	121
9. Adjust Your Perception & Pay Attention to Your Self-Talk	133
10. Kindness, Patience & Knowledge	145
11. Kismet & Creation & Be What You Seek	163
12. Gratitude, Love, & Wisdom	175
In Closing	193
My Gift for You	196
About the Author	197
REFERENCES	198

Chapter 1

Expand Your Reality
Transform Your Circumstances

"Reality has a sliding door."
Ralph Waldo Emerson

It was a beautiful, sunny afternoon in late spring in St. Paul, Minnesota. I headed out on a mile walk from my home to where I was meeting a friend at his work. From there we were going to a movie. I wore a strappy lavender and white checked sun dress and strappy white sandals, each crisscrossed and woven with eight thin straps. I'd walked about four blocks when above the over-arching trees the sky suddenly turned a dark greenish-grey. A mountainous thundercloud rolled overhead like a bizarrely inappropriate stage prop wheeled out during the most bucolic moment of a performance.

Determined to get to my destination before rain fell, I stepped up my pace. A weird stillness dropped all around. No birds, no breeze, no sun, no people, no traffic. As if I'd slipped into another dimension. Undaunted—or slightly daunted, but with unflinching determination—I hurried a couple more blocks and was now equidistant between home and my destination, when a little old lady stepped out on her porch and called to me melodramatically I thought at the time, "Girl! Come into my house! There's a tornado coming ... *come in!*"

I paused. Not because I considered her invitation or bothered to think about what she said, but because I was inflexibly polite. "No thanks, I've only got a couple blocks to go," I exaggerated, not wanting her to worry about me, a stranger. I waved, smiled, and scurried on, while she, anxiety etched on her face, returned into her house. I walked another block. It started to rain. Or, more precisely, it began to plop erratic, huge, dollops of water from the sky. Most of them missed me, but when they hit, it felt like someone dumped half-a-cup of cold water on me. I walked faster.

Then the world changed.

An intense pressure pushed on my ears and a low, strange hum, that I felt more than heard, came from everywhere. I was alone in the middle of the city, with not a person, dog, cat, or bird anywhere. Suddenly, I was glued to the spot and could not move. A wind swirled around and around, wrapping my sun dress about me like the tight husks around a young ear of corn, and as I stood, pinned, the gigantic, ancient trees lining the sidewalk in this charming craftsman architecture-influenced neighborhood began to crack and drop gargantuan branches around me in a great whirling circle. Leaves, dust, debris flung about so that all I could do was close my eyes and brace myself as much as I could.

I *prayed!* "Please let me stay right here with my feet on the ground." Was it minutes? Was it seconds? I have no idea, but before long, the intense pressure subsided, and I felt I could move. I opened my eyes, smoothed back my long hair swirled around my face, and looked about to see that indeed, not only branches, but also trees were down all around. It was as if I had stood in a bell jar, unharmed. Happily, the houses also appeared to be intact. The path of the tornado went right down the middle of the street—at least where I was.

I took a step but was inhibited by something at my feet. Looking down, I saw my beloved strappy sandals with every single strap pulled out from the base of the sandal, only held on by the tiny buckle and thin strap around each ankle. I took what was left of my sandals off and hurried, barefoot, tip-toeing around debris, the remaining distance to my friend's car repair shop, while the sky opened up and soaked me to my very bone marrow.

Needless to say, my friend sitting in his auto repair shop, without electricity, in the dark with a transistor radio and flashlight registered shock when I came through the door, bedraggled, soaked, barefoot.

That experience definitely expanded my reality.

I was only eighteen and very open to learning. During the event, I was simply *there*, my senses taking in all the improbabilities, just—*learning*. Not until afterwards did I realize the immensity and the bizarreness of it. I had grown up in Nebraska and had seen and been very close to many tornados. But I'd never been outdoors *in* one.

Expanded Reality

Probably few people have. All I needed was a little dog in a basket to complete the metaphor of making art, life. Or is that making life, art?

Consider with me a few of the ways in which my reality became expanded:

- I realized I was made of stronger stuff than I'd had occasion to previously observe.

- Prayer is powerful.

- Don't wear strappy sandals when going to go for a walk in a tornado.

- But I think the most profound expansion of my reality was an awareness, an understanding, that I was as big as a force of nature. Or, more to the point, that I *was* a force of nature.

Because, while the event transpired, I was not frightened. I was full of exuberance, full of the thrill of the tornado. It was as if the tornado was sentient and in my awe and my forgetting of self, I came into the tornado's exuberance, the delight of the elements in tearing around like a behemoth Id-driven three-year-old child.

That thrill of life was tantamount to a visitation. In that moment when I prayed for my feet to stay on the ground—*and they did*—I was bestowed a gift of strength from the shaman-like energy of the tornado.

> *"Gather strength from life's storms."*
> **Jonathan Lockwood Huie**

However! I'm not suggesting that you chase tornados until one catches you in order to expand your reality. Expanding your reality is a personal matter. It won't to be the same for any two individuals. Maybe I was being particularly inaccessible to my higher self at the time, and it required that degree of sound and fury to get my attention.

Perhaps you are accessible through more subtle means.

Let us agree, you and I, that you are willing to explore the idea, the concept of expanding your reality—with an intention of finding your path and engaging your purpose. Let's further agree that this is something you're willing to be open to even in the most mundane of experiences.

> *"Your sacred space is where you can find yourself again and again."*
> ***Joseph Campbell***

Discovery

We embark on a quest that will have numerous discoveries. The first leg of this journey of discovery is for you to contemplate where you are today, and how you got here. You might begin by asking yourself the following questions:

• When I am successful, what are the actions and events that have contributed to my success?

- What holds the truest meaning in life for me?
- Are there changes I'd like to see in my life?
- What makes me laugh absolutely spontaneously?

What do I hold sacred?

> *"The business of becoming conscious is ultimately about asking yourself 'How alive am I willing to be?"*
> *Anne Lamott*

Transforming Your Circumstances

In the process of expanding your reality, you are likely to encounter another experience—that of transforming your circumstances. We all encounter things that hold us back or appear to keep us down.

What is something that holds you back or keeps you down?

A common approach with something that keeps us from our goals is to go around and around, repeatedly doing battle with the same old dragon.

But another approach is to simply step *over* that old dragon and move on. It *is* possible to have a quantum leap in one's growth, a spontaneous quantum leap.

I've worked with hundreds of people who have walked into a corner or fallen into a hole, metaphorically, where their lives seem to be stuck.

An example I'll share was one sweet sixty-two-year-old man, Joshua, who had, due to a variety of life reversals, moved in with his daughter and her boyfriend. He came to see me because he felt his daughter needed help. Her relationship with the boyfriend was turbulent and miserable.

"I pointed out to Joshua that *he*, not his daughter, had come to see me and I couldn't do much about people who were not present, but I felt that he and I could discover some things that would make him happier.

> *"You can't make much of a difference in things*
> *Until you change yourself."*
> *Alice Walker*

Somewhat reluctantly, he agreed to let me pursue my line of thought. Why was he reluctant? Because he felt he didn't need counseling.

This is the point at which I get to launch into my oft-repeated commentary on there being nothing wrong with asking for insight and psychological support. Our emotionally fragmented and disenfranchising society has foisted upon us the notion that we must be able to "go it alone" or there is something wrong with us, which is pitiful, if not down right mean.

Tribal people have always had someone to go to—a shaman or elder—to help sort things out and get a better perspective on expanded reality. But in our contemporary society, many people live in a virtual emotional vacuum.

Back to Joshua—over time he came to see the good points in what I had to say and made small shifts. He started out working on, and understanding, his frustrations rather than continue his an endless loop of blaming others for his unhappiness.

We talked about how his choice to respond with negative emotions was precisely that—a *choice*. I suggested that if he began to consciously choose more positive and empowering emotions, solutions would materialize.

"If you were to set aside the current dynamics of being very unhappy living with your daughter and her boyfriend, and instead decided to transform your circumstances, what would that look like?" I asked him. "What would be different?"

Joshua answered without hesitation, "Well, I wouldn't live there."

"Okay then, let's approach your life from that perspective."

> *"You must do the thing you think you cannot do."*
> *Eleanor Roosevelt*

"I can't, because of my finances."

"We're not saying, 'I can't' right now. We're looking at transforming your circumstances. This starts with 'I can.' So, honoring that thought, let's look at the picture of where you would like to live when transforming your circumstances."

Joshua proceeded to humor me, picturing the perfect place he'd like to live—or at least as much as he could allow himself to picture it, while still resisting. When this—our third—session was over, I suggested he figuratively put on his hat and jacket, because he had done some very clear picturing and what he'd manifested was moving toward him as he moved toward it.

To get to the punch line, he'd moved into a charming cottage with front and back yard, and with numerous other details just as he'd described in my office, in under a month.

> *"Life shrinks or expands according to your courage."*
> *Anais Nin*

In my experience of working with people, such seeming miracles are not unusual.

I've observed again and again that when someone is willing to transform circumstances, transforming circumstances arrive.

I dare you—I double dare you—to try it. Cost of admission is free, you have nothing to lose, and much to gain.

> *"We must travel in the direction of our fear."*
> ***John Berryman***

The Challenge: Responding, Not Reacting

> *"Respond; don't react.*
> *Listen; don't talk.*
> *Think; don't assume."*
> **Raji Lukkoor**

As mentioned earlier, we all encounter things that hold us back, or keep us down. A common way to deal with impediments is to repeat patterns we've used before. But remember, a definition of insanity is to repeat the same behaviors, or to have the same reactions as we've had before, *expecting a different result.*

To get different results, begin now to imagine different behaviors (different causes produce different effects). Picture yourself responding rather than reacting. When we take a couple of moments to respond rather than immediately react, those few seconds of thought sometimes give us the room in which to make the choice *not to respond at all.*

Let's look a bit more at the difference between a reaction and a response.

Consider the word: Re-Action. The same action occurs again. This situation is not going anywhere if the same thing that is acted by A is then *re-acted* by B. The problem cannot get out of its own way.

A reaction is hair-triggered. It boomerangs back. A reaction augments disagreements, and causes all parties to become more and more entrenched in their position, whether right or wrong. Reactions are not constructive, the only goals they reach are unhappiness and alienation.

Sometimes, if not often, we react without even hearing correctly, or not listening to the whole comment, cutting the other person off because we assume we know what is being said.

A *response*, however, provides the opportunity for new, clarifying, helpful, reasoned and tempering information to be introduced. A response comes after a moment of respectful reflection for both you and the other person. Upon reflection, you are able to make a response that honors the people and the discussion, even if you disagree with the other person's position.

As you can see, responding allows you to make calm and meaningful observations, while informing the other of your differing opinions and beliefs. Or, taking a moment to consider the disagreement, you may discover that the other person is correct, or has valid points you hadn't considered before.

Person A may or may not accept your position, but you at "B" have given yourself choices. There's a better chance of a positive outcome, including agreeing to disagree.

Conversely, you may realize it's not constructive to continue the conversation and that it's wise to politely remove yourself from the situation altogether.

You will break the bonds that constrain you when you lay claim to the key that unlocks the bonds. The key is within you. Reach inside and free yourself.

> *"It's not because things are difficult
> that we do not dare,
> It is because we do not dare
> that things are difficult."*
> **Seneca**

Your Part:

Expanding Your Reality,

Transforming Your Circumstances

> *"There are no circumstances that clever people
> Do not extract advantage from."*
> **La Rochefoucauld**

Where are you now in relation to your true heart's desire, and in relation to your Life's Purpose? If you're reading this, I believe you're tantalizingly close. But you may feel you're not "*there*" yet.

It may not even seem that you're all that close. It may frustrate you that your heart's desire appears about as close as, and is less clear than, the horse-head nebula. Okay then, let's close in on your nebula. What shapes up as we approach?

First, I encourage you to open your channels of belief. Above all else, believe in yourself.

As you work your way through the following "filling the glasses" self-insight exercise, you may see some interesting—and perhaps surprising—information about yourself unfold. This information begins to answer the question you may be asking of how to believe in yourself. *DO NOT* fuss with or second guess your answers. Just move right through the exercise, trusting the intelligence in your "gut." Your gut (self-intuition) knows you better than anyone, anywhere.

When you expand your reality, you will come to imagine that it might not only be okay if you pursued your heart's desire, but that, to be true to yourself and to everyone who's life you touch, you *must* manifest your heart's desire (aka: Life Purpose).

Why? Because this understanding comes from your deepest internal knowing, it issues from that which you unconditionally love. And that which we love is both known and unknown to us. The part that is known is comfortable, a blankie through the long, stormy night.

The aspects of love that we are less aware of excite, inspire, and intrigue us, lighting up the imagination. It ignites your intuition and hooks you up to your higher self and to the all-abiding creative force.

Picture Transforming Your Circumstances and Expanding Your Reality

Imagine you are standing in a beautiful park—surrounding you are gigantic trees. You can see a small patch of beautiful blue sky far above. You can also see the edge of a lake, little song birds, a squirrel.

What if you found yourself in the top of the tallest tree, looking out? Now you see many more trees, a huge, glorious sky, both sides of the lake, hundreds of song birds flitting about, and the herons and ducks and geese in the lake. You see the eagle's nest in the next tree. Off in the distance, you see the far horizon and the curvature of the earth.

You've transformed your circumstances and expanded your reality. You see more, you know more, and you feel more with the added input. You therefore can appreciate more.

When you transform your circumstances and expand your reality intending to honor your life's purpose, you'll discover that you move from a place where the view is limited to a view that is much expanded. Hopes and dreams you've had about your heart's desire have more opportunities to become realities. Your potential takes on a clarity and logic that appeared unavailable at "ground level."

> "If you can dream it, you can do it."
> **Walt Disney**

It's not until you're in the top of the tree that you see the appropriate place for the eagle's nest, and it's not until you engage your courage to expand your reality that you see where your abilities can fully blossom.From the tree top you see, spread out below you, more choices and more opportunities, you experience greater joy, tranquility, and peace. Serendipitous events come to you and you are open and available to them. Your understanding is broadened.

When you put courage into action, fear fades away. Your abilities and your talents come to the front.

> *"Everyone has been made*
> *For some particular work*
> *And the desire for that work*
> *Has been put in every heart."*
> ***Rumi***

"How do I transform my circumstances and expand my reality, with the goal of finding myself in the midst of my Life's Purpose?" you may be asking.

Here are some concrete answers, along with concrete attitudes and actions you can begin to utilize:

1. Do what you love and love what you do

Love has the ability to expunge self-doubts, lack of clarity, and confusion.

> *Love has no doubts*
> *Love is clear*
> *Love is never confused*

2. Be filled with gratitude

Every breath you take is a miraculous gift. Be grateful for every moment. When you are filled with gratitude, that for which you are grateful multiplies. When you are thankful, more of what you are thankful for is drawn to you. Live consciously and trust yourself, your insights, and your intuition.

3. Trust serendipity

An intentional mind draws to it serendipitous responses everywhere in your life, whether work, play, or quiet times, while gratitude helps you notice when what you're looking for has arrived.

4. Consciously decide to trust what comes into your life

Conscious, creative beings call their circumstances, their opportunities, and their blessings to themselves.

5. Encourage & nurture optimism, joy & peace

These consciously affirmed emotional states—optimism, joy and peace—keep the train of your intention solidly on the tracks of your personal growth. They contribute to your expanded reality and your transformed circumstances.

How Full Is Your Glass?

Following are several rows of glasses. Put a mark on each glass, from empty to full, and write a number from 1 to 10 by the glass to indicate the amount of fulfillment you experience in your life regarding the named aspect.

Write the positive events, actions, thoughts and feelings in the glass below the line that fill the glass to that point, and write above the line anything that is not at present in the glass that would make it a "10," or that is preventing it from becoming a "10."

Example: I draw a line on Physical Health above the middle and write "7." Below the line I might write "yoga" and "good diet" as things that contribute to my health, and above the line I might indicate "knee injury" that affects my physical health.

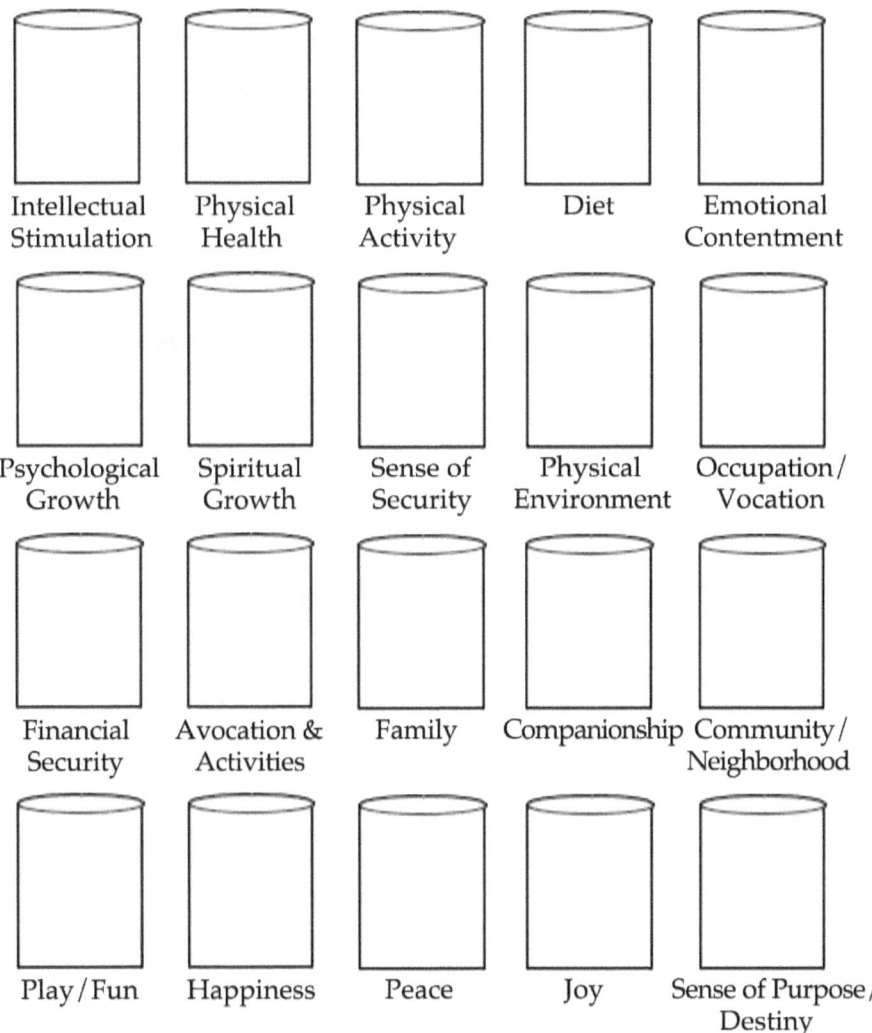

Getting Clarity

Now that you've finished filling all your glasses and indicated the positives and the negatives contributing to each, draw a line down the middle of a sheet of paper and list any of your glasses that are at "5" or below in one column and the ones that are at "9" or "10" in the other column.

Then rank them in order of importance *to you*.

We're looking for the places you would like to change, and those areas that are strong and that you desire to maintain.

Example: Let's say Avocation & Activities is a "4." You may have other items "5" and below, but Avocation is first on your list of the areas you'd like to change. Then rank the other "5" and below items.

With the items you've numbered "9" and "10," rank the one you are most satisfied with as "1," followed by the others in order of your satisfaction.

Getting to the Nitty Gritty

Pick an area you'd like to focus on first while working your way through *Finding Your Path, Engaging Your Purpose.* It can be any area regardless of how you ranked it. The foregoing exercise is a barometer, letting you get a pretty clear picture of your path at present, and giving you insight into your purpose.

Write *three small goals* regarding the area you'd most like to improve that you're willing to implement in the next three months:

1. _____

2. _____

3. _____

Write *three larger goals* regarding this choice that you'd like to see manifest in the next year:

1. _____

2. _____

3. _____

What would the glass have in it, or not have in it, in order to be rated a "10"?

_____
_____
_____

What would it take to bump it up two points during the next eight weeks?

_____
_____
_____
_____

Chapter 2:
Imagination, Creativity, & Genius

> *"What is now proved,*
> *was once only imagined."*
> **William Blake**

Imagining

Imagine you wake up tomorrow morning and the first thing you do is exactly what you would like to do. Then imagine that the second thing you do is also exactly what you would like to do. Imagine, in fact, that you move through your entire day, sailing like an elegant tall ship through calm water, sails unfurled, doing precisely what you desire to do, and accomplishing everything you intend to accomplish.

There is something you know, there is an awareness you have, that is unique—only you know it, only you have your particular perspective and understanding. You've come into this life by a Creative Force that granted you the breath of life, and thus you became *who you are*. Energies await, passively humming, anticipating your imagination's engagement with them, which will fuel your heart's desire and your Life's Purpose.

Don't get in the way of your creative forces with time-wasting, vitality-burning issues. Move forward into the full flowering of your imagination. This is the link between you and the web of existence. Quantum physicists and contemporary philosophers are writing and talking about the energetic web that composes everything. What science has previously called "space" is now understood to be filled with a pulsing, web of intelligence.

> *"Imagination is more important than knowledge."*
> *Albert Einstein*

Everyone is a part of that web, which includes your web. Now, for the sake of visualization, consider that your web has nodes where every strand of your web intersects with another and forms a node. Picture these nodes energizing and lighting up, opening to allow knowledge and wisdom to pass through for the benefit of yourself, for everyone, and for everything.

Dr. Wayne Dyer observed that imagination is "the God within you." Imagination visualizes the ingredients necessary to manifest the creation you're working on and pulls them together from the web of existence in a form which is unique to your creative abilities. When you rely on your imagination, the channels of creativity open up and clear the path that brings your creations into physicality.

Creating

> *"The root meaning of the word 'art' is: 'to fit together' —*
> *Each time we fit things together, we are creating."*
> **Corita Kent**

An important "secret" to creating (not really a secret at all), is your willingness to visualize your project as already created. Get on with your life as if your heart's desire is present now—as if the details you are attending to are simply tying up the ends of something that is already realized. Why? Because this takes the stress, the anxiety, the negative "what ifs" out of the picture. Also because—as you will read more than once in this book—*Thoughts Become Things*.

Here's a way of making this work: Contemplate something you've accomplished in the past.

Do you still wonder if it'll manifest? No. It has already been done. Do you have stress and anxiety about aspects of it you must attend to? No. Again, because it is already done.

While thinking about this, you might stir up the stress and anxiety you felt about it in the past and if so, you can see how unnecessary those energy-tapping feelings were and are—they don't get the job done, they get in the way of getting the job done. Accomplishing each step as it arises gets the job done.

Now bask for a moment in the glow of accomplishment and fulfillment that resulted from that previous successful completion. Then bring those positive feelings into the present moment, directing them at the creation you're now manifesting. That is to say, align your emotions with your picture of your current creation having been completed.

Don't mull over what's missing! Mulling—a form of contemplation—equals "bringing into being," and you do not want to bring into being more of what's missing. When imagining and creating, picture positive, successful results.

For instance, if a person says, "I don't have money for this project," the focus, and therefore the energy, is on "no money." Instead say: "resources for this project are on their way and will become available as appropriate." This allows the interconnected web to send energy to fulfilling your intention.

> *"There is no greater joy*
> *than that of feeling oneself a creator.*
> *The triumph of life*
> *is expressed by creation."*
> **Henri Bergson**

Setting Aside Time

Let me share a personal example of visualizing what I'm creating as already completed.

I'm writing this on a lovely, balmy Friday morning. And because I'm enjoying listening to all the song birds and my pet geese chatting, chirping, trilling and singing with a pulsing, living rhythm—to an extent where I'm enticed now and then to pause and listen, I well up with gratitude for my amazing sense of hearing.

I'm writing longhand with a ball-point pen on the backs of recycled paper, so no machine comes between the sounds of nature and myself. I am also holding the sensory image in my brain, heart, mind and emotions that this book I am writing is completed and published and if I were to walk into my library, I'd see it with a handsome spine, sitting on the shelf. That visualization makes *this* moment of *that* future reality relaxed, fun, joyful, intriguing, healing, meditative, affirming and peaceful—because I'm writing a published book. As such, the writing is more exciting—it's a page turner, because I'm so curious to discover what I wrote next.

The time-space continuum is an illusion we've all agreed to sustain, a context to play, learn, grow, wonder, and muse within. So there's no reason not to play with it. Time is a subjective concept. You've no doubt had experiences of *time* when it went sloooowwwwww, and times when time went *fassssssst*.

I can collapse—or remove—time and appreciate both the contemplation of the published book on the shelf at the same time as enjoying the process of writing the book amid bird song and sunshine on a bucolic spring morning.

I'm filled with peace and pleasant, anticipatory excitement. I experience joy, happiness, and love for my miraculous fingers and my brain that drives my fingers—seemingly automatically! My mind delights in engaging the machinery of my brain, vertebra, discs, shoulders, sinew, muscles, bone, arms, elbows, forearms, hands, thumbs and fingers that all allow me to manifest a book on the shelf in the other room, in libraries, in other people's homes, in other languages, on recording devices, and so forth, some time in the near future.

In this way I share my intention
Driven by imagination
Shaped by creativity
Inspired by the power of the moment
And sparked by the pilot light of my vision.

Genius-ing

> *"One is not born a genius,
> One becomes a genius."*
> **Simone de Beauvoir**

Visualize shifting your thoughts to the energy of light. The higher energy of light moves into harmony with intention. Here genius resides.

There is something you've thought, something you've imagined, something you've created in your mind, a way of understanding that only you perceive, imagine, or understand, no matter how many billions may populate the planet. In the process of changing your habits of thought to allow for the expansion of your thinking on the web of intention where genius resides—as suggested by de Beauvoir's quote—you give your unique understanding an opportunity to thrive.

This "web of intention" is waiting for you to believe—if you do not already—in your genius. When you hook up with the web of intention, or, more correctly, the Web of Life, its power will assist you in bringing into being your heart's desire.

Consider again your connection with the Web of Life and the nodes that energize and light up when you become actively engaged, becoming open channels of positive, creative, loving energy instead of blocked energy. You productively initiate your own potential, while allowing this energy to flow through you, helping others find their path and engage their purpose.

Nurturing Your Genius

Nurture your genius by:

1. Simplifying your life

2. Being contemplative

Positive contemplation is to the flower of genius as sunlight is to the rose. Pay attention to your insights and intuition, honor and nurture them.

Anxiety, poor self-esteem, self-judgment and envy are weeds that cause counterproductive habits of thought, and have no place in your garden. Keep them weeded out.

"Genius ... the faculty of perceiving in an unhabitual way."
William James

Practical Application

Let me share a story about Delores. She was working in one of the two mills in the community where I live, it being two little mill towns joined together, each originally centered around its own mill. A single woman without children, she was making good money. But she had wisely come to the realization that money was not everything.

The first time she came to my office, she started out by saying, "I want to do something more meaningful with my life,"

"What would be more meaningful?" I asked.

"I want to work with children. I want to make a difference in young lives. I'd like to help kids discover what inspires them and encourage them to do what they love. Like never happened for me.

"When I was a kid, I was told I'd grow up and work in the mill. *And that's exactly what happened!* I hated the idea when I was little, and I despise it now. But of course, I can't just up and do whatever I want."

"Why not?"

"Because even if I dared to quit my job, I have no credentials to teach."

"Let's set aside all these negatives you imagine for the time being and study the positives. Let's consider your:

- Imagination
- Creativity
- Genius

Let's talk about those."

I soon learned that Delores had already put all three into practice. She was instrumental in creating new games, developing lessons, and organizing social events for the Sunday School class she taught.

I suggested she look into taking elementary education classes. Since she was on a "shift work" schedule, which in a mill means the work schedule is always in rotation where workers work days, then evenings, then nights, there would be classes she'd miss. But she and I talked with her instructors and, given her determination, all of them were willing to work with her regarding the few missed classes if she stuck by her commitment, and fulfilled her assignments. On occasion she was able to go to a different section of a class, sometimes her instructors met with her one-on-one.

The bottom line was, because of her perseverance and passion for her goal, the strength of her heart's desire, the fearless application of her imagination, creativity, and innate genius, she soon had a part-time job with Parks and Recreation, organizing events for kids. She also began to teach a couple of creative classes through Community Education.

During that time she had saved money from her well-paying, unfulfilling job, and was able in a year to quit that job, go to college full time and keep very happily busy with that and her part-time Parks and Recreation and Community Education jobs. In addition, she earned educational credits toward her degree for her Parks and Recreation activities.

A beautifully successful outcome!

Everyone has imagination, creativity, and genius. When you honor them and apply them, believing in yourself, nothing can stop you!

The Challenge: Control Issues

In a strange twist of fate, it sometimes happens that when people have gotten on their path and are making good progress in the direction of their intention, up pops all types of "brain noise" about why they ought not make the wise moves that will allow them to become better acquainted with their genius and develop their imagination and creativity.

These interferences can be control freaking disruptive. Trying to control everything and/or everyone, i.e., "control freaking," occurs, *when a person feels out of control.*

Here are some ways control issues show themselves:

1. Attempting to direct other peoples' activities, behaviors and beliefs. This typically only succeeds in causing people to distance themselves. On another hand, people who are subject to a control freak—especially children—may become crippled and unable to effectively run their own lives.

2. Control freaks are so preoccupied with trying to control events, or to prevent events that have

not even happened and that may *never* happen, that they do not live in—and therefore don't engage in, enjoy, or appreciate—the present moment.

3. The efforts of control freaks to manipulate their own lives as well as the lives of others causes the boundless pleasure of living in the moment—*the power of now*—to be overwhelmed and set aside.

Becoming aware of these habits is the first step in beginning to change them. Throughout **Finding Your Path, Engaging Your Purpose**, you will find tools and ideas that build up your self-confidence, and assist in disempowering control issues.

Your Part:
Imagination, Creativity, and Genius— Your Golden Eggs

Do you find yourself feeling frightened when reading (or if someone says to you), "You have genius—use it?"

Okay. Take this moment to be scared. Now be done with that.

Don't get in the way of your creative forces by nurturing poor self-esteem. As mentioned, that which science used to call "space" is now proving to be filled with a pulsing, and apparently intelligent, web, or net.

There is no point in fearing anything, because you cannot *fall*. You will simply land on the embracing, supporting net of All Being and All Knowing. You cannot *fail*, as there is no failure. There are only innumerable learning experiences.

As Thomas Edison said when asked what it felt like to fail a thousand times in attempting to invent the light bulb: "I never failed once— we now know a thousand ways not to build a light bulb." That's the attitude that produced the light bulb.

Does that insight make a light bulb turn on *in you?*

> *"Failure is the condiment that gives success its flavor."*
> **Truman Capote**

Keep your creativity and imagination in motion. This "grows" your genius. Develop projects to keep all those synapses in the brain firing at optimum productivity. One way to keep the brain active is to work on problems. Become a Sherlock Holmes in imagining the next and best action you will take to solve a problem. Let's try this process right now. Think of a problem you're dealing with and write it down:

_____
_____
_____
_____
_____
_____
_____

Now, write five ideas, ways, and/or actions that address solving this problem. *Do not* over-think your answers! Ask the question: How can

I solve this problem?" Quiet the mind. Then write down what comes.

Wacky ideas are fine. They're great, actually. Often, the off-the-wall thought is precisely the best solution. Also, letting "crazy" ideas float to the top of the mind clears out thoughts like, "I'm going to have the wrong answer," "I don't like how this feels," or "I won't do it."

So, here goes, five ways to solve this problem, off the top of your head:

1. _____

2. _____

3. _____

4. _____

5. _____

Now begin to put those problem-solving answers into action!

*"Genius finds in our everyday words
The music of the woodland birds
Discloses hidden beauty furled
In the commonplace stuff
Of the everyday world."*
Charles Frederick Johnson

Chapter 3:

Clarify Your Intention & Cast Out Your Doubts

"Our intention creates our reality."
Wayne Dyer

Clarify Your Intention

What is your intention? Somewhere in you there's a picture, an image, a perception, of your intention. Somewhere in you, you know your Life's Purpose. If you were to truly commit to thinking, feeling, and knowing your Life's Intention—without low self-esteem, without second guessing, and without the ever-present noise of what I call "the-rat-in-the-squeaky-wheel-in-the-back-of-the-mind"—I believe you would do everything in your power to bring your Life's Purpose into being.

The-rat-in-the-squeaky-wheel-in-the-back-of-the-mind grinds away. Its din shuts out your heart's desire, your intuition, your gut-level knowing (which is generally accurate information, although it can be extremely difficult getting that information into your conscious mind).

Once you've named your:
Intention
Life's Purpose
Heart's Desire
It's time to:
Cast out Doubt

Cast Out Your Doubts

Doubts are where "second guessing" really gets obnoxious.

Let's look at some of the roadblocks we can come up with. Have you ever heard any of the following from yourself?:

"Who do I think I am?"

"'They' are going to find me out."

The twin stoppers:

"This has already been done, so I shouldn't do it."

And:

"No one's ever done this before. I must be wrong. I shouldn't do it."

"Where did I get the idea that I could do this on my own?"

"Who's going to help me?"

"I'm not worthy."

"If I put this in motion, I'll have to be responsible for it."

"Even though I'm not now doing what I love, what if I do this thing that I think is my heart's desire, and it turns out I don't love it?"

"I'm afraid I'll learn something I don't want to know, so I'll just stay in the dark."

"What if I do this and it's a success, I'll have to attend to it."

"What if I do this and it's a failure, I'll be embarrassed, hurt. I'll affirm so-and-so's (spouse/parent/friend/self) belief that I can't do it."

"As long as my heart's desire is but a dream, I always have my dream."

> *"Change is inevitable, growth is intentional."*
> **Glenda Cloud**

Let's ban these doubts one by one, and quiet that squeaky-wheeled rat.

1. "Who do I think I am?"

You are an amazing, miraculous and impeccably manifested being! Even your perceived imperfections are part of your perfection. That which you think of as imperfection is the energy source you may tap into, to drive you forward to your intentions. It's the irritation of the sand that makes the pearl.

And so the question morphs into: "Who do I think I am, allowing doubts to get in the way of my Life's Purpose? Who do I think I am, daring *not* to do it?"

2. "They are going to find me out."

They who? Find out what? And even if so— *so what?* We think we aren't "qualified" to know what we know. We second guess our truest pictures of self-manifesting. Perhaps we imagine there are those who are out to do us in. Never mind. Even if this is true, "they" do not have to answer to your Higher Self ... *you do.*

If there is something you know, or there's something you have an urge or energy around manifesting, the only tragedy is in not doing it.

3. "This has already been done."

Once again, so what? Many people will buy the same dress pattern, but no two dresses will be the same. A room full of artists may all paint the same bowl of fruit, but no painting will look like the others.

4. "No one's ever done this before, I must be wrong/mistaken."

Or maybe you're onto something the entire planet is waiting for. Do not be judgmental of the creative energy flowing through you. Get your negative thoughts out of the way and let the energy flow. If everyone let this negative thought rule, we'd still be living in the dark because we'd never have figured out candles, let alone fire. Let alone electricity.

5. "Where did I get the idea that I could do this on my own?"

If you don't do it, who will? What if you ignore your calling and after a while someone else comes up with it (as is often the case with an idea who's time has arrived)? You'll only be able to say, "Why didn't I move on my insight when it first came to me?"

6. "Who's going to help me?"

Zen proverb:

- "When the student is ready, the teacher will come."

Also:

- "When the teacher is ready, the student will come."

7. "I'm not worthy."

Don't waste time and energy on this autobiographical, noisy and unnecessary, ancestor-based thought. Put it down. R.I.P.

> *"Each of us is born with the potential for the unfolding of our true self. When you deviate from the truth, you are interfering with the intention of something greater than you are—call it nature or a higher power. As a result, you develop discomfort."*
> **Anonymous**

8. "If I put this in motion, I'll have to be responsible for it."

Yes. And if you *don't* put it in motion, you're responsible for it. Once your intention has called upon you, you cannot be "uncalled"—you can only be unresponsive/irresponsible. If you try to stop up your senses and your knowing, you'll just get energetically constipated.

9. "Even though I'm not now doing what I love, what if I do this what I think is my heart's desire, and it's not?"

If you're not now doing what you love and loving what you do, you are not in your . Don Juan taught Carlos Castenada to be aware of and to honor his "Place," which is good advice for us all. Make movement—move toward that which you feel is your heart's desire, your "place."

And remember ... *remember your heart's desire.* Remember your true calling. Remember your intention. Remember your Life's Purpose. This knowledge is in you. Clarity manifests as you move.

If you move into what you believe you'll love, and you discover it's not what you love, you'll have made forward motion. You'll begin to allow the next level of self-awareness, wherein you're likely to discover what has been waiting for you all along.

Allow yourself to grow!

> ***Movement is drawn to Clarity***
>
> ***Clarity reveals your Heart's Desire***
>
> ***Heart's Desire leads to Movement***

As long are you are the engineer (ego), your train (higher-self), and your tracks (subconscious), will synchronously move toward your intention. Anything or anyone else in the engineer's seat (doubt/addictions/co-dependent relationships, etc.), will have you derailed.

10. "I'm afraid I'll learn something I don't want to know, so I'll just stay in the dark."

Fear is your companion in the darkness where you're hiding. Come into the light. The more you know, sense, feel, and understand, the more you're in the light. Fear is banished.

Here's what's truly wonderful—the more you move into the light, the more light *you become*, casting out doubts and fears for yourself and everyone your light shines upon.

11. "What if I do this and it's a success, I'll have to attend to it."

Yes. That's correct. Let me repeat an above statement: Once your intention has called you, you cannot be "uncalled"—you can only be unresponsive/irresponsible.

12. "What if I do this and it's a failure, I'll be embarrassed, hurt. I'll affirm so-and-so's (spouse/parent/friend/self) belief that I can't do it."

Again, there is no failure. Why not look at this in Edison-like terms? If a new thought doesn't come together right out of the gate, it's not failure, wrong, or a mistake. It's simply a way not to do it.

Sometimes when having learned it doesn't work to do something one way, you have the insight that it's an excellent way to do something else.

This is the process of genius and is frequently the impetus of inventions.

13. "As long as my heart's desire is but a dream, I always have my dream."

If you only assimilate the following from this chapter, you'll be well on your way to Casting Out Doubts and Clarifying Your Intention:

You will always have a dream. The more you come into your Life's Purpose, the more your dreams—which are imaginings from the Creative Source—will come to you and through you.

Creativity, whatever it may be; arts, healing the human family, caring for creatures, urban planning, cooking, baking, planting a garden, improving government systems, so on and so forth—flows, and the ideas grow exponentially as you keep centered in your being. This creativity then expresses itself through your heart's desire, life's purpose, and creative inspirations. That is to say: Your Dreams.

"Live with intention. Walk to the edge. Listen hard ...
Play with abandon. Laugh. Choose with no regret ...
Continue to learn. Do what you love.
Live as if this is all there is."
Mary Anne Radmacher

The Challenge: Victim Energy

There is no longer time nor space in your life for being a victim.

People who allow themselves to be victims can never come fully into their personal development potential, as they have already chosen not to own themselves. Giving your power over to a victimizer or victimizers means you're allowing someone else to write your script, which overwrites you finding your path and getting on with your purpose.

Also, keep this in mind: people who allow themselves to be victims are often, themselves, victimizers, even if oblivious to the fact.

We all need to decompress on occasion, but victims are people who have a litany of woes without hope of reprieve, blaming their unhappiness and lack of success on someone or something else. Or many someones and somethings else. Don't blame circumstances or others for your state of being. Learn from them, and move forward into your personal autonomy.

Yes, sometimes events are out of our control. But curtail the inclination to become a victim in response to life's challenges. Release compromising, victimized emotions. Victimization and self-pity have no positive influence on external events, while negative, reactive emotions take a huge toll on you.

"There is always a certain peace in being what one is, In being that completely."
Ugo Betti

An approach to succeed in untying the bonds of being a victim is to practice forgiveness. Although this may sound counter-intuitive, true forgiveness will pull the rug out from under the attachment the abuser has on you.

Holding onto abuse by maintaining self-pity, resentment, covert anger, poor self-esteem, codependence, enmeshment, and lack of forgiveness is how you *become* a victim, and *continue* to be a victim.

The practically mystical power of *forgiveness* allows you to set all of those negative emotions and mind-sets aside, and come smiling into your domain of productive self-confidence.

Your Part:

Clarify Your Intention and Cast Out Your Doubts

Write down two of your doubts, perhaps from the list above, or others of your own, then write a paragraph or two that casts out that doubt.

Doubt #1: _____
_____
_____
_____
_____

Banishment: _____
_____
_____
_____
_____

Doubt #2: _____
_____
_____
_____
_____

Banishment:_____
_____
_____
_____
_____
_____

*"The key to abundance
is meeting limited circumstances
with unlimited thoughts."*
Marianne Williamson

Chapter 4:

The Future is NOW!
Learn to Think from the End
Be Receptive to Change

> *"You hit only what you aim at.*
> *Therefore, aim at something high."*
> **Henry David Thoreau**

The Future is Now

Roger came to me when he got laid off work. He was a construction worker, and had been on and off employment, which is not unusual for construction workers. But it had reached a point where he couldn't stand it anymore.

I asked him, on a scale of 1 to 10, how much he enjoyed his work when employed. He said it was about a five.

Although it's often like pulling teeth to get people to explain why something important in their lives only rates a five, I persevere. This is what I finally got out of Roger: he was no longer in his thirties, and construction work was hard work, often in cold rain, which was miserable, and hard on the body. But, on the other hand, he said, he'd had a lot of great work experience, and he knew as much or more about his work than most of the foremen he worked for.

I found Roger charming, intelligent and candid, and I believed his assessment of his skills and knowledge were no doubt accurate.

I asked him, "what would you most like to do professionally?"

He hesitated, but finally said, "I'd really like to be a materials manager, the person who gathers all the details about the materials that are needed for a job. But I never seem to be able to get away from hard labor."

"Have you ever specifically pictured yourself in the role of materials manager?"

He answered sheepishly, "I do sometimes find myself fantasizing about it, but I cut myself off when I realize I'm doing that."

"Why?"

"Because I don't think I'll ever get there, and because I have this idea that I'll drive it away if I think about it, as if I deserve it, or something."

"Of course you deserve it! Why wouldn't you deserve it? The very best way to bring it into being is exactly what you've done—picture it. But you must believe in yourself."

"It takes as much energy to wish as it does to plan."
Eleanor Roosevelt

Thinking from the End

Then we launched on an exercise of *Thinking from the End*, where first Roger saw himself fully engaged in his purpose, just exactly as his Heart's Desire painted the picture, and although it took some coaxing and coaching, here is the essence of Roger's picture:

"I see myself in my home office. When I don't need to be onsite, I'm able to work at home. I have all the equipment I need to do my job around me, telephones, computers, etc.

"I have a very comfortable chair and a beautiful Oriental carpet of deep blues and reds at my feet. I've installed a large picture window in the room that becomes my office in my home, and I have a beautiful territorial view of the countryside and the river.

"I work for several companies and I always have more than enough work. In fact, I even have to turn down jobs. I'm respected and earn that respect by taking full interest in every job I take on.

"I'm continuing my education by taking some night courses. I actively network and I also connect other people to one another when it's an advantage to them."

With this wonderful picture in mind, we embarked on the "working backwards" process.

"What has to happen *just* before that complete picture?" I asked.

"Well ... put in the picture window," he said teasingly.

"I think you're right! Let's write that down. What has to happen just before that?"

"Probably getting the equipment, the computers and a phone system, that I don't even know anything about right now."

"Okay, and what before that?"

"Taking some college courses."

"Excellent!"

We worked our way backwards to the then present moment, where the first step he affirmed was necessary was to get a blank book to write down what we'd discussed, and transcribe his "Thinking from the End" notes.

The next step was to write the entries in the reverse order so that the first step came first, and so forth to the result, leaving space for the dates each step was embarked upon and when accomplished.

> *"Planning is bringing the future into the present so that you can do something about it now."*
> **Alan Lakein**

I also suggested he write his *Thinking from the End* notes on the right page, leaving the left page blank for notes about things learned, things to research, observations about what processes worked best, phone numbers and other information about contacts along the way, and for mini *Thinking from the End* breakouts.

As Roger moved forward with his Heart's Desire, he was surprised to discover along the road that companies he'd worked for as a contract construction worker had paid attention to him. He was not invisible like he'd thought. They had observed his reliability, his hard work, and his intelligence, so when he began to apply for Materials Manager positions, the groundwork he'd already laid served him well.

We also discussed the probabilities that as he moved through this process, some of the steps might change in order, or importance and that what initially appeared to be one step, when encountered needed to be broken down yet further into a mini or subset *Thinking from the End*. A good example of this was the process of taking classes, broken down into where he was going to go, getting the catalog, determining which classes and when, talking with an advisor, etc.

Building Bridges

It's a good idea to keep in mind that we are always building bridges, we are always laying groundwork.

Within a mere nine months Roger was beginning to work occasionally in his oriental-carpeted home office.

> *"All you need is the road map, and the courage to press on to your destination."*
> ***Earl Nightingale***

When you think from the end and clearly map out the end result—whether large or small—working your mind-pictures back to the present in small steps, you then have that map, written out with clear directions from the "You Are Here *" spot to the Heart's Desire Destination.

As you travel, the map may be altered, or built upon, or streamlined, as is the case of almost any journey. But having the map, the clear pictures, the affirming words written down so that even if you have days when you feel compromised and not sure of your progress, you can see the progress you've definitely made, you can see what is written down as the next step and simply take it.

Just take the next step—you will make progress. If the next step seems inaccessible, break it down into a mini Thinking From the End.

> *"When you make a choice,*
> *You change the future."*
> ***Deepak Chopra***

Being Receptive to Change

The single most relevant factor in Roger's success in arriving at his Heart's Desire was his acceptance and willingness to *be receptive to change.* He neither allowed any poor self-esteem issues, which, like most of us, he did have, to shake him off his path, nor did he allow any entitlement concepts keep him from taking each step, each action, in turn.

> *"The first step toward change is awareness.
> The second step is acceptance."*
> **Nathaniel Branden**

Next, after picturing, writing, and affirming your Life's Purpose in the framework of intention, be receptive to change, be receptive to new information. Be open, peaceful, and centered as you go about your life. In your mind and in your emotional body behave as if what you claimed as the fulfillment of your Life's Purpose is your current state of being. As if it is *NOW*. Your intuition will inform you of your creative, manifesting power.

It's not necessary to push, or be self-critical.

There's no space for "control freaking" while allowing your vision to manifest. Your highest, truest purpose, your clearest path, needs no pushing or control efforts. While keeping your vision of your Heart's Desire clear, contemplate every experience you've ever had and everyone who's ever been in your life.

Consider, for a moment, that all you would judge good and all that you would judge bad has been the objective of your higher self for you to glean insights and to learn from each of those experiences. Imagine that the goal has been to get you to this point at this moment, for the purpose of this insight, in order to become aware of *this particular Intention*.

Your life has always had a purpose, and now that you are conscious of that fact, you can release anything which does not contribute to your highest potential. That is to say, consciously engage your free will in this goal.

The more you work with this manifesting energy, the more, I believe, you will learn that everything is supported by a Divine Intelligence, which is not separate from us, but is, indeed, the very essence of each and every individual.

The Challenge: Entitlement Issues

A few words here about entitlement. Entitlement is the process where we feel we're "owed" something.

It's important to realize that entitlement is crippling.

I was recently talking with a friend who had taken a job working with welfare recipients. In her wide-ranging work experience, she'd previously been employed at vacation resorts where the population she worked with was wealthy and privileged.

"I took this job to help people," she said. "I'd gotten fed up with dealing with the entitlement issues of wealthy people. But guess what? It's been shocking to discover how much I have to deal with entitlement issues with people on welfare. Every day I listen to people tell me what they deserve and what they ought to get because they're poor. It's the exact same litany I used to hear in resorts, except people went on about what they deserve and what they ought to get because they're rich."

We all have likely had occasions in our lives when we've felt entitled to something. But candidly, no one and nothing owes you or me, or any of us anything, "just because."

We make choices and decisions, and end up where we are as a result of those choices and decisions.

> *"Once you make a decision*
> *The universe conspires to make it happen."*
> ***Ralph Waldo Emerson***

There is a low grade anger (often subtly displayed as being "too nice," or not being able to say no, or being overly self-effacing, as well as simply flat out being defensively angry) that is attached to entitlement. This makes sense, because if we feel we are owed something—"just because" (because I'm poor, because I'm rich, because I'm disabled, because I'm married, because I'm divorced, because it's Tuesday, because I say so) then we're going to be peeved as a general mood. *Just because.*

Think about this: It's quite challenging to be happy and to manifest your Heart's Desire if, underneath it all, there's a nearly hidden, grinding, peeving, sense of entitlement. A sense that you don't have to do what needs to be done to become self-fulfilled because someone or something owes you.

Roust out entitlement thoughts, expose them to the light of reason, letting them dry up and blow away.

Again, the only person, entity or energy that owes you anything is yourself. All the other particulars of people and events are simply a series of blessings.

Entitlement's Behavior

Be willing to take a hard look at yourself and see if you must admit that you've done any of the following. *Be honest!*

Here are some ways entitlement can express itself:

• Complaining about what one ought to receive instead of what one did receive.

• Passing the baton of abuse by abusing innocent others in the way one pictures oneself to have been abused.

• Or conversely, if the abuser is still in one's life, figuring out ways to abuse the abuser (revenge).

• Taking physical gifts, or gifts of time and attention, for granted without gratitude or sincere thanks.

• Not apologizing when appropriate.

I suspect we've all done some of these things at some time. Apprise this behavior, replay the event, and rewrite your part in the script.

Picture how you would *respond* rather than *react*.

Feel empowered about how you'll now handle any of these challenges.

In this "new and improved" frame of mind, it's easier to be receptive to change when entitlement issues have been removed. When you are receptive, you are peaceful and centered. You enjoy allowing whatever comes upon the pond of your reflections to share its information with you. It's a pleasure to see revealed what you've been working on, on your journey to your Heart's Desire.

Your Part:
Learn to Think from the End & Be Receptive to Change

> *"Make a plan. It wasn't raining when Noah built the ark."*
> **Richard C. Cushing**

How do you bring your Heart's Desire, which is currently not in physical form, into four dimensional (three dimensions of space, one of time) reality?

Becoming fully self realized means having clarity about your intention. Become crystal clear regarding your intention.

First, produce the picture in your mind of the result of your intention. You now begin (if you haven't already) to have the intellectual and emotional experience of what your Heart's Desire—your Intention—looks like and consists of when it is fully manifested, which is the process of *Thinking From the End*.

To assist you in this process, start by promising yourself that you will be completely open and receptive. You begin with your inner Intention, and then move into the process of engaging the Universal Power of Intention, an entirely neutral force.

Think of the Universal Power of Intention as a great vat in which all the materials for all of creation, in any and all dimensions—dimensions and possibilities which you and I cannot even begin to imagine—this vat is a mind-boggling toy box, mad scientist's lab, builder's tool box, where every tinker toy, Lego block®, Lincoln log, DNA, molecule, atom, energy force that-is-was-or-could-be—resides.

Picture yourself coming to this vat/toy box/lab/tool box, where you see the potential of every dream you ever dreamed. It is all there for you to manifest your Heart's Desire. All you need to do is believe in, and move on, your Intention.

Your manifestations come into being when your intentions bring you joy, peace, and happiness.

Begin to write about your intention by *Thinking from the End*, the point of manifestation:

1.) When my Heart's Desire and my Intention are realized, this is what I see I've manifested:

_____
_____
_____
_____
_____

2.) When my Heart's Desire is realized, I see that I am (where are you? what are you doing?):

_____
_____
_____
_____
_____

3.) This is what I feel about this state of full/fulfilled self realization:

_____
_____
_____
_____
_____
_____
_____

4.) What I am observing relates to my Life's Purpose in—

    a.) Emotional Terms:

_____
_____
_____
_____
_____

    b.) Psychological Terms:

c.) Spiritual Terms:

Affirmation:

From this point forward, I affirm and acknowledge the process, power, and energy of the synchronicity that I have put into motion. I affirm that there are no accidents. I live meditatively and mindfully, releasing energy around obsessive control (which can never have the view or the knowing of Cosmic Intelligence).

As I energize my intention and set it in motion, I must release it, like a carrier pigeon. It is not possible for the "energy pigeon" to manifest and retrieve what I wrote in my message of fulfilled intention, if I hold onto its all-knowing wings.

"Plan your work, then work your plan."
Norman Vincent Peale

Entitlement

What do you feel someone, or society, or the universe owes you (your answer may be wide ranging)?

For example, perhaps you feel your father or mother or spouse or ex-spouse or child or friend owes you an apology. And perhaps they do. But you need to release it back to them and not own it any longer. Holding onto entitlement around something that has not happened, and may never happen, is likely to bring about a transfer of that entitlement issue to someone else in your future.

If you have an ex-spouse who was abusive and who never apologized, and you (perhaps unconsciously) feel entitled to that non-forthcoming apology, a friend or a new significant other will come in the line of fire of your expectation of that apology. If you don't allow closure on events, they continue to fester.

Release the past, release all anger, release all entitlement feelings and issues. Move forward, embracing your Heart's Desire.

Write below an entitlement issue you are ready to release:

_____
_____
_____
_____
_____
_____
_____

Affirmation:

I release (examples: spouse, mother, the Universe) _____ from my feelings of entitlement and any notion that "they owe me." I claim that I will feel peaceful, happy, and joy-filled as a result of this release. I will feel "lighter" in my emotions and in my general spirit. My interactions with others will be clear and enjoyable, and everything in my life will simply "fit together" better as a result of this release.

I believe that replacing my thoughts around entitlement with the energy of unconditional love is the highest and best means of healing.

GOOD WORK! Pack in life's suitcase your highest and best ... leave the rest!

Chapter 5:

Believing & Behaving "As If" Embracing Abundance

> *"People who say it cannot be done should not interrupt those who are doing it."*
> **Author Unknown**

Believing & Behaving "As If"

In the previous chapter I wrote, "go about your life as if your Life's Purpose is your present state of being. As if it is now."

Thinking, feeling, believing and behaving as if your Life's Purpose is currently engaged eliminates thoughts and emotions that are limiting and compromising. Acting "as if" stops you from putting conditions or "yeah, buts" on your commitments.

If you are motivated—every day—by a clear, and ever clearer picture of your work, your calling, your purpose, because your attitude is that this is where you are, not that it's where you might be, somewhere, somewhen else.

When we act "as if" our intentions are currently manifested in our lives, the seeds will begin to germinate, becoming a reality in your physical world. When you plant cucumber seeds, you do not get tomatoes.

Don't place conditions or limitations on your intentions. Does the mighty evergreen, ever contemplate the notion that the tiny seeds in its pine cones will not produce trees? No.

Every bit of nature responds to its nature, manifesting its destiny without compromising its productive abilities. Take this lesson from nature.

> *"Keep your thoughts positive,*
> *Because your thoughts become your words.*
> *Keep your words positive,*
> *Because your words become your behaviors.*
> *Keep your behaviors positive,*
> *Because your behaviors become your habits.*
> *Keep your habits positive,*
> *Because your habits become your values.*
> *Keep your values positive,*
> *Because your values become your destiny."*
> **Gandhi**

There are many Olympic contenders who, when interviewed about their successes, say some variation of "I saw myself performing exceptionally, clearly in my mind beforehand."

"Keep away from people who try to belittle your ambitions. Small people always do that, but the really great make you feel that you too can become great."
Mark Twain

The clarity of mental pictures, without room for doubt, without mental chatter, without looking back, second guessing, comparing, or criticizing, causes the germination of intention to sprout. Believe it already carries you to the moment, as the moment rushes to you when it bursts forth in the material world.

"Both abundance and lack exist simultaneously in our lives, as parallel realities. It is always our conscious choice which secret garden we will tend. When we choose not to focus on what is missing but are grateful for the abundance that's present, the wasteland of illusion falls away and we experience Heaven on earth."
Sarah Ban Breathnach

Feeling Abundant

Another belief that is supportive and helpful in bringing your intention into being is affirming abundance.

Is not the Universe abundant? Is there anywhere you can turn and not be amazed by the abundance and miracles that surround you? How did that little, charming house plant come into being? How miraculously contrived is every single leaf.

Many people share with me their "Moments of Epiphany" when something just *HIT THEM* that this condition we call "life" is miraculous.

A friend told me of when he was living in Brazil, and everything around him was a verdant, fecund rain forest. He began to think about the intelligence that knew to put poison in a snake's hollow fangs so that the snake would bite and poison, in one graceful move, efficient and miraculous, and he was awash with the awareness of creative intelligence.

This shifted his skeptical, scientific, intellectual reserve to a deep knowing that there is an overseeing intelligence.

> *"Thoughts are boomerangs,*
> *returning with precision to their source.*
> *Choose wisely which ones you throw."*
> **Author Unknown**

A client recently told me of her epiphany when contemplating her skin. "How amazing an organ," she said, "that my skin lets sweat out, but 'knows' not to let water leak in."

Can we feel anything other than abundant? We are soooo abundant! The supreme intelligence that is the very essence of the cosmic web which shows us again and again and again that there is more abundance than we can ever even tap, while we sometimes go blindly and ungratefully through life, not acknowledging its wonders and abundance, let along engaging fully in it.

> *"Like attracts like.*
> *Whatever the conscious mind thinks and believes*
> *the subconscious identically creates."*
> **Brian Adams—"How To Succeed"**

Abundance has nothing to do with money. Money is only a symbol that we've all agreed upon to manifest as a means of either understanding our lessons, making progress with our growth, and be engaged in our life's purpose, or to not understand our opportunities, while we bemoan not having enough money.

Look inside yourself and see the poverty thinking in your paradigms if you feel you do not have enough money.

Acknowledge the abundance in your life, shaken down and flowing over! Knowing your life is abundant, affirming that you are in the place of your Heart's Desire, which is a way of saying you are successful, will contribute to your ability to detach from things—which opens up the gate through which they readily flow.

Imagine being as wise as skin,

Knowing what to let out,

And what to let in.

The Challenge: Equanimity—Balance

"The word 'happy' would lose its meaning if it were not balanced by sadness. It is far better to take things as they come along with patience and equanimity."
Carl Gustav Jung

Let us consider the concept of equanimity. Balance through all life and all life experiences is exceptionally challenging for us all on occasion, even if one person's challenge is another person's shrug. But whatever poses a challenge, you are supported in the calm of equanimity.

Out of equanimity manifests peace of mind and a calm, centered sense of well being, which contributes profoundly to engaging one's purpose.

*"Let the wave of memory,
The storm of desire,
The fire of emotion,
Pass through
Without affecting your equanimity."*
Sri Sathya Sai Baba

Your Part

Go for a walk and contemplate how incredibly rich you are. Your eyes and ears, your hands and feet are priceless!

> *"Walk as if you are kissing the earth with your feet."*
> **Thich Naht Hahn**

Walking meditations are an ancient tradition in eastern spirituality, and for good reason. Nothing clears out brain fog, energizes the body, calms and inspires your emotions, and nurtures your spirituality like going for a walk, especially in nature. Getting yourself into nature on a regular basis will ground you in equanimity.

It's also excellent to go for a walk right in your neighborhood if you don't live in or near nature. Take in your surroundings, say hi to a neighbor or two. Plus, it's always uplifting and will make you smile to have a chat with a local cat or dog or squirrel.

It's important to change your environment on occasion. In the calmness of a mindful walk, insights arise. Clarity around something you've felt blocked about may well flower like the lotus.

"Walk slowly—This is a kind of invisible practice. Enjoy nature and your own serenity."
Thich Naht Hahn, "How to Walk"

Write about an insight or an experience you had while going for a walk:

_____
_____
_____
_____
_____
_____

Chapter 6:
You Are a Part of Everything
&
How to Attract What You Desire

> *"Whatever is going on in your mind is what you're attracting."*
> **The Secret**

You are a Part of Everything

There is power in understanding that you are a part of everything.

Lynn McTaggert author of several remarkable books including The Field, discusses some points quantum and mechanical physicists are coming to understand. For instance:

1. "Human beings, and all living things, are a coalescence of energy in a field of energy connected to every other thing."

2. "In the *Zero Point Field* (which is) the microscopic vibrations in the space between things ... the very underpinning of our Universe is a heaving sea of energy."

3. "Living beings are packets of quantum energy constantly exchanging information with this inexhaustible energy sea."

So, if you are intrinsically a part of all unified energy—*and you are*—you cannot fail, as all growth, when pursued with intention, adds to your learning experience, even those aspects which you had not anticipated, or that didn't turn out as expected.

Intention is supported, on one hand, by a clear picture of a goal, but is balanced, on the other, with an attitude of allowing. Letting go. Being a part of everything means you release resistance and you move away from issues of control. In order to keep a clear picture of your goals, and to be in the center of engaging your purpose, an attitude of allowing is a handrail on the path.

There is an exercise in self-help groups where one or two people stand behind a subject. The subject falls backwards, in pure trust that she will be caught by the others.

How much more supportive is the entire web of existence? If this were not true, we would not even be here. Trust your place in being a part of everything.

Sometimes what having that trust requires is building up your self-esteem. Listen to your negative self-talk and remove it. Phrases such as "stupid me," "I'm an idiot," "I don't know what I'm talking about," and so forth have no place in your vocabulary. You are a part of everything, and as such, you have your place and function.

> *"Self-esteem comes quietly, like the truth."*
> ***Amity Gaige***

The character Hugo in the movie by the same name said something to this effect: "I think of the world as a big machine and I know that to work, a machine has just the right amount of parts. If I'm here, a part of this machine, I am not an extra part. I am needed and I have something to do."

You are needed and you have something to do. You are a part of everything. Love yourself, believe in yourself, and engage your purpose. When you are in a state of allowing, you release resistance.

Examining the Characteristics of Resistance

Resistance is usual among people who experience the illusion of a need to be in control.

Resistance is experienced by individuals with poor and/or harsh self-esteem.

Resistance is a major factor with people who allow themselves to be either victims or victimizers (or, as is often the case, both). As previously discussed, people who own victim energy can never come into their fullest personal development, as they have already chosen not to own themselves.

Resistance is characterized by doubt and a negative outlook. Doubt and negativity are fueled by notions of being separate/separated from everything, and most certainly an illusion of being separate from unified energy. But no one and no thing is separate from unified energy.

Shifting Your Beliefs

So! If it is true that you are intrinsically woven into all of unified energy, you cannot fall, you cannot fail.

If you decide you are going to make a shift in your belief system, and this shift is away from control, away from victim energy, away from fear, you will discover that your path becomes more and more clear, that your purpose already has its motor running, waiting for you to put your will into gear so your purpose can get on the road.

This is a good moment to pause and take stock of what you've attracted into your life thus far. If you feel poor, unhappy, depressed, unclear, confused, anxious, bored, guilt-ridden, unsure, self-and-other-critical, judgmental, unloved/unloving, and/or as if you don't own your life—ask yourself what you've done and what you've thought to bring these circumstances into your life.

Then change your thinking, change your behavior.

If you feel poor and unhappy, study the wonder of something—a sunset, a kitty, or simply sit eyeball to eyeball with yourself in a mirror and study your own amazing eyes, or close your eyes and study the back of one hand with the fingertips of your other hand, holding the thought of how miraculous and amazing ALL LIFE is. After that, go ahead and be unhappy and depressed, if you dare, if you can. But ask yourself, "what's my payoff for being unhappy?"

Life is relentlessly miraculous! It's difficult to remain depressed when you're filled with the wonder of miracles.

"There are only two ways to live your life. One is as though nothing is a miracle. The other is as though everything is a miracle."

Albert Einstein

If you feel fuzzy and unclear and confused, do some Brain Gym®, which can synchronize your body and brain for better focus, comprehension, communication, and emotional health.

Or get Donna Eden's book, **Energy Medicine**, and practice a few of her mind-body hook-up movements. Lack of clarity is due to not engaging or "hooking up" various parts of your brain with the rest of your brain. Indecisiveness may seem overwhelming, but it is a choice to allow it to rule your roost. Take a few drops of wild oat tincture (generally available at your local health food store), which assists in clarity, focus and determination.

But most of all, affirm to yourself that you are staking a claim of ownership upon your own clarity.

If you're anxious or bored, become physical on a regular basis. Being physical releases anxiety and boredom. If "an idle mind is the devil's playground" (and I would suggest our demons are of our own making), then what that devilish energy is doing with idleness is developing anxiety and a sense of boredom.

When we are engaged in our purpose, there's no time to be bored or anxious.

Release guilt, as guilt is an emotion wherein you permit others to dominate you. It's a profound waste of energy. Don't feel guilty and don't attempt to make others feel guilty. Guilt's henchmen are manipulation, criticism, and being judgmental. Guilt nurtures feeling unsure and insecure when trying to second-guess what the other person wants of you. *But!* Have you ever noticed that you can *never* jump through someone else's hoops to their satisfaction (nor can they ever jump through your hoops to *your* satisfaction)?

All of this is an unpleasant, guilt-driven muddle that leads to feeling unloved and unlovable. When a person feels unloved, *they become unloving*. So you can see that the "false emotion" of guilt has many negative repercussions. It needs to be excised!

Attracting What You Desire

Every moment of every day, we are attracting to ourselves the experiences that occur in our lives.

1. We're making clear, conscious decisions that have unambiguous results.

2. We're making subtle choices that over time produce an outcome.

3. We're having subconscious thoughts that are attracting to us events and experiences.

4. We're choosing emotions that forcefully and magnetically draw to us energies in which events transpire.

The first of these is pretty straight forward, and it's fairly easy to see how it's true. It's 2 through 4 that gives us our challenges if we're not attentive.

If you have a goal, if you desire to engage your purpose, all four layers of your ability to manifest must be in concert. Your subtle choices need to be in line with your conscious decisions.

Let's look at an example:

1. A person enrolls in college.

2. She takes classes that are not of particular interest to her because she thinks that's what's expected of her.

3. She tells herself she's not bright enough to get through college because she can't become engaged in her classes.

4. She considers herself a failure, becoming depressed when she does poorly, seemingly confirming her negative self-judgment.

5. She becomes involved in a relationship that further interferes with her self-esteem and goals.

This is but a sketchy example of how our lives might not unfold as we desire, due to our own choices.

Let's look at the example when someone is aware of the layers of attracting what one desires and keeps it all focused in the same direction:

1. A person enrolls in college.

2. She takes classes that are of particular interest and relate to her particular skill sets.

3. She tells herself she's excited and happy to be fulfilling her goal of getting a college degree.

4. If she gets a poor grade, she learns what she did not know, and is happy with the experience of learning.

5. She does not let anything or anyone interfere with her goal.

If she has someone in her life who is antagonistic to her goal, whether jealous, possessive, belittling, or for any other reason, she re-evaluates that relationship to determine if she may need to establish distance with that person.

REMEMBER: You can never jump through someone else's hoops to their satisfaction. You can never "make" someone else happy. That is a decision each one of us makes, individually, in the privacy of our own heart.

Our lives are made of what we've attracted to us by the four above-named processes, which are worth repeating:

1. Conscious decisions
2. Subtle choices
3. Subconscious thoughts
4. Chosen emotions

A Story with a Happy Ending

I had a client with a job she absolutely despised. Not only did it not tap into her intelligence and creative brilliance, but she was on the "wrong side of the table" every day. And every day it ground deeper into her sense of self how far she was from where she desired to be—even though, literally, she was very close.

She was the "lunchroom lady" at a middle school. But all she wanted to do was teach a class she had imagined where the children would integrate dance, movement, art, writing and performing skits into a united whole, no holds barred, allowing the children freedom to explore their creative abilities individually and in cooperative groups.

Her vision of this workshop was clear, but she had one block she perceived as insurmountable. She had only 3 years of college, so did not have a bachelor's degree, let alone a maser's degree, and she believed she would never be allowed to teach with that limitation.

She had #1 of the four processes—making a clear, conscious decision—down pat. But in the way of her goal becoming realized, she:

2. Held the belief that she was not "good enough" because she didn't have a degree.

3. She would never be able to be anything other that the "lunchroom lady."

4. And daily she allowed herself to be depressed about her job and her life.

We worked together on the understanding that she was an integral part of everything, that her vision would make the world a better place, and that she ought not block that beautiful vision.

Why not, I encouraged, begin to put some wheels in motion, starting with not choosing to be depressed? Why not look at the children in the lunchroom and picture teaching them in her workshop? She agreed to give it a try. This one shift in her choices changed her world view within a week.

Then we brainstormed what avenues she might go down to make her dream concretely come true. Long story short, within half-a-year she was giving quarterly weekend workshops that were overwhelmingly successful and had a wait list, that gave her fulfillment and joy. The reality was better than her dream.

She didn't mind her job so much, as she looked forward to the next workshop and what she might do to add to it. Before long two other school districts picked up her workshop, and she quit her "lunchroom lady" job.

Huge, unanticipated bonus, I suggested she query local colleges for credit for her workshops, her preferred college gave her a resounding "yes!" With only a small handful of courses she took online, she had her bachelor's degree in under a year.

The Challenge: Guilt

Why is guilt so challenging? Because guilt is attached to an internal mechanism, not the external event.

I've observed many times, when working with people, that they allow themselves to be held hostage by guilt. They seem to believe that they have to be as perfect as God. But they are frustrated because they see themselves as a god who goofs up a lot.

They claim the ownership of guilt to events, circumstances, conversations, and so forth, that are not theirs to own. That is to say, these events, circumstances, and conversations belong to someone else. But you will hear guilt-ridden individuals, when owning that which is not theirs, apologizing, relentlessly. And then, when they don't get absolution—and they never do, because even if the other person says, "that's okay," or "there's nothing for you to feel sorry about," or "it's not your fault"—the guilt-owning individual will not relinquish it, and does not access peace.

Whereupon the guilt-owner feels self-pity because "nobody understands me," when perhaps everyone around him understands him better than he understand himself.

> *"I once tried to figure out the first time I felt guilt, and it goes so far back that I might have been an inch long at the time."*
> **Lee Marvin**

What a great quote, expressing the pervasive nature of guilt! Of course, a one-inch zygote has nothing to feel guilty about. But guilt will, like a parasite, take up residence where it's neither deserved nor wanted.

Running around and around on the guilt-pity track is a powerful distraction from getting on with the business of finding your path and engaging your purpose.

Just let it go! Stop feeling guilty, stop feeling pitiful. You don't have time to be off your path with this non-productive energy that interferes with your full self-realization.

Your Part

Learn to recognize these thoughts and emotions as distractions on your path:

Guilt
Anxiety
Boredom
Unhappiness
Feeling unsure
Poverty mind-set
Unloved/unloving
Critical/judgmental
Fuzzy/unclear/confused
Not at the helm of your ship

Put these thoughts and emotions down, turn them around, and kick them out the window. Stop attracting what you do not desire. Start fresh with a clean slate (or sheet of paper) and write down what you consciously intend to manifest in your life.

Consider your goals and/or desired manifestations, and write down some of your thoughts regarding the following:

1. Conscious decisions:

_____
_____
_____
_____
_____

2. Subtle choices:

_____
_____
_____
_____
_____

3. Subconscious thoughts:

_____
_____
_____
_____
_____

4. Chosen emotions:

_____
_____
_____
_____
_____

A quick litmus test about guilt—how many times a week do you say "I'm sorry," or feel you ought to apologize? Learn to hear yourself say, "I'm sorry," or any of its clones. How many of those occasions are ones you are directly responsible for?

How many of them actually have nothing to do with you, or were due to circumstances outside of your control? (By the way, none of this refers to saying, "I'm sorry, *but* ..." which is an entirely different emotional stance altogether. It's sarcasm and is untruthful. A person is not the least bit sorry with the phrase, "I'm sorry, *but* ..." Guard against using this phrase!)

Be aware of the following circular logic starting with saying "I'm sorry," and *break the cycle at the outset*:

"I'm sorry"=
"No one understands me" =
Self-pity =
"I'm unlovable" =
"I'm bad" =
Feeling guilt =
"I'm sorry"

Write an affirmation that lets you release the power of guilt. Example: "I am willing to correct my errors. It's not necessary for me to feel guilty. Once I've done what I can do to better a situation, I release it and move on. If I realize that I'm saying 'I'm sorry' for something I've not actually had anything to do with, I release it immediately. I am consciously breaking the habit of automatically saying 'I'm sorry."

List 5 ways in which you see and understand that you attract what appears in your life:

1. _____
_____
_____

2. _____
_____
_____

3. _____
_____
_____

4. _____
_____
_____

5. _____
_____
_____

*"If you believe it,
You can achieve it."*
W. Clement Stone

Chapter 7:
Release What Others Expect of You
&
Do No Be Aggrieved

To free us from the expectations of others,
To give us back to ourselves —
There lies the great, singular
Power of self-respect."
Joan Didion

Release what Others Expect of You

Does it seem likely that you will be able to come into your own highest personal manifestation, or become fully engaged in your purpose, if your attention is divided by focussing on the expectations of others?

The further you move along your path, the fewer are the travelers. Therefore, in order to engage your unique purpose, you will likely discover that you put down what others expect of you.

By the way, when I say "unique purpose" that's not to say your purpose isn't shared by others, but it is to say that you are the only person who can do what you can do. Of the billions and billions of snowflakes, no two are exactly the same. How much more true, then, is this for humans? And how much more exponentially true for the smaller population who are becoming awakened and who have embarked on the journey of engaging their purpose?

If you try to please everyone and attempt to fulfill the expectations of others, you simply attract more and more of what others expect of you. You are reduced to the lowest common denominator of all the people whose expectations of you, you are trying to fulfill or appease. You lose yourself, your will, and your heart's desire.

You'll not be able to find your own path, as what you encounter are all the crossroads of everyone's path, tromping under their dusty self-serving needs the clarity of your individual path. Your purpose fades into nothing.

Keep your focus on your intentions—what you intend to create and manifest with your precious life and your special gifts. Even if your purpose is to help others, the needs of others only have clarity in the terrain of your path.

> *"I don't measure myself by others' expectations*
> *Or let others define my worth."*
> **Sonia Sotomayor**

In my private practice, I've occasionally seen that people who say that all they want to do is serve others, in the end, are often actually calling out to others to heal their own wounds. They are willfully in the victim role, which attracts victimizers (or, in the case of parents, they socialized their children to be victims). Then the victims victimize the co-dependent and enmeshed self-named helpers. Why? Because they have not engendered the internal courage to find their own path and engage their own purpose.

No matter where your path leads, you are the one determining its course. Therefore, you are the power source for fulfilling only your own expectations. No one else is in your skin. No matter how loving someone else's agenda may be for you, only you are you. No matter how giving and helping your purpose, you must develop, honor, and attend to the melody your Heart's Desire sings.

While laying claim to the clarity of your expectations and releasing the expectations of others, you're likely to hear negative, critical, belittling and otherwise hurtful comments from those whose expectations you have released. One's "tribe" is companionable and relevant, but moving away from tribe on your own vision quest, unprescribed by them, can elicit condemnation and shunning in a variety of ways.

Strengthen your resolve. Others are not on your journey, and they are not responsible for your journey. You are. Criticism and shunning are small when compared to engaging your purpose. It may not seem like it while going through the experience, but in hindsight, you will see this is true.

Do No Be Aggrieved

> *"We should be too big to take offense and too noble to give it."*
> *Abraham Lincoln*

Feeling aggrieved or offended is an extremely weakened position. When you take offense at someone's comments or behavior, you:

1. Give them your power

2. Feed their negative energy

3. Nurture their erroneous notions that they have a right to have power over you.

When you're offended, you are often reacting to the other person being offended.

Let's say that you have someone in your life who, when you get together, all he does is complain—complain about work, his boss, his wife, his friends, the grocery store clerk, so forth and so on. To listen to him, there is simply nothing positive in his life.

He has an expectation that you will listen, and you've trained him to believe this by listening to his complaints in the past. Further, you've encouraged his picture to look for the downside in his life by reinforcing his "complaint litany."

Let's say that you are choosing to no longer fulfill his expectation that you will support his negative outlook. So you tell him, "we all need to vent on occasion, but I'm no longer willing to support your overwhelming negative outlook."

There's a good chance that his reaction to your comment will be to express offense. He retaliates by offending you. He may say something like, "What's the matter with you?" or "Are you suddenly too good for me?" or "Ever since you've been on this 'Finding Your Path' kick, you've been a real pain in the neck" or "It's all about you, isn't it?"

If you react to his offense by being offended, the downward spiral has won a round.

Respond don't react. Transcend to the place in you where even if his zinger hits your ouchie you remain on your Path, in Peace.

Residing in peace in your higher awareness is the greatest healing balm for yourself, and is, therefore, what you share with others. As you move away from the place where wounded people can access you, hurt you, or irritate you, you will discover your integrated Self.

You'll become inspired to be there with your integrated Self more and more, until you realize that it's time to put your name on the mailbox, because it has become your permanent residence.

The Challenge: Blaming

> *"When you cast blame,
> You disempower yourself
> And relinquish control
> Of your destiny."*
> **Kirk Charles**

Sentences that begin with, "I can't or I haven't gotten on my path....

because my husband_____

_____

because my children _____

_____

because my job_____

_____

because my physical condition_____

_____

because (fill in the blank)_____

_____

are *BLAMING STATEMENTS*. There is no room on your path for blaming, passing the buck, victimization, pity—or any of their cousins or shirt-tail relatives. These are choices you're allowing yourself to make which limit or derail your progress. *REFRAME THEM.*

We all need to decompress on occasion, but victims are those who often, if not generally, have a litany of woes without a silver lining in the clouds anywhere. They put the blame for their lack of success and their unhappiness upon someone/something else. They insist it's someone else's fault that they are victims.

I receive a daily meditation called "Messages from the Universe" (you might want to sign up for them, they come from Mike Dooley:

theuniverse@tut.com

One day *"The Universe"* said something to the effect, "When I see someone saying, 'He keeps getting in my way,' I see someone making excuses."

You don't need to make excuses, you don't need to blame. You need to be on your path and engaging your purpose.

Reframing

What is "reframing?" It's the process of hearing and attending to negative, disempowering statements, and rewriting or re-wording them to become positive.

Let's look at an example with the statement: "I haven't gotten on my path because my husband has let me know that he does not approve of what he refers to as my 'selfish-self-improvement craze.'"

In the process of reframing you ask yourself any questions that come up about the blaming statement, such as:

1. Is it true that my claim to finding my path and engaging my purpose is a temporary fad?

Answer: No.

2. Is it selfish to become all that I'm meant to be?

Answer: No. Quite the opposite. I'm contributing to the raising of consciousness of humanity when I take responsibility for myself.

3. Am I required to have my husband's (or anyone else's) approval in order to get on my path?

Answer: Decidedly not. My mirror tells me I'm responsible for my growth.

4. Are there perhaps other reasons I have hesitation about getting on my path?

Answer: Yes.

5. Such as?

Answer: Insecurity, unsure of myself, fear, frustration, laziness.

6. Do these answers lend insight into why I might think to blame someone else for the choices I'm making?

Answer: Clearly, yes.

7. Am I able to set aside this blaming statement and reframe it as a positive affirmation?

Answer: Yes.

Original Statement:

"I haven't gotten on my path because my husband has let me know he does not approve of what he refers to as my 'selfish-self-improvement craze.'"

Reframed Statement:

"I will move forward on my self-improvement path, knowing that it will contribute to my being productive, happy, and at peace, while, at the same time, contributing to raising the consciousness of humanity. I'm aware that my growth will make those around me who do not want to budge, uncomfortable. But their disapproval is their issue with *their* growth and *their* responsibility. I claim the power of my intention, I release all blame, and replace it with unconditional love.

> *"Praise loudly,*
> *Blame softly."*
> **Catherine The Great**

If you're committed to your path, no excuse will interfere with your determination.

Your Part

Recall two occasions when you tried to fulfill someone else's expectation of you that were not your own:

1._____
_____
_____

2._____
_____
_____

Recall two occasions when someone offended you:

1._____
_____
_____

2 _____
_____
_____

Recall two occasions when you have blamed someone else for your choice not to lay claim to your growth:

1._____
_____
_____

2._____
_____
_____

Now reframe at least two of the foregoing six sentences into positive affirmations. Maybe you'll discover you'd like to reframe all of them—good for you! You might want to keep all the interim questions that lead to your reframed affirmation. It's possible that your series of questions leading from a negative statement to a positive affirmation have nearly universal applicability in your life.

1._____
_____
_____

2._____
_____
_____

3._____
_____
_____

4._____
_____
_____

5._____
_____
_____

6._____
_____
_____

Chapter 8:
Have Respect for Yourself
Lay Claim to Personal Strength

Have Respect for Yourself

"Self-respect cannot be hunted.
It cannot be purchased.
It is never for sale.
It comes to us when we are alone,
In quiet moments, in quiet places,
When we suddenly realize that
Knowing the good, we have done it,
Knowing the beautiful, we have served it,
Knowing the truth, we have spoken it."
Whitney Griswold

How can you discover your highest purpose if you don't feel worthy? And yet, how can you possibly not feel worthy? You are the absolute perfection of your Creator's imagination, unique and exquisitely manifested. There is not a wart or cowlick that has come into being without intention.

Don't be judgmental, but see the beauty in that which we may have contrived as imperfect. Stop attempting to outguess or critique the knowing energy which put all of creation into motion and get into creating and manifesting motion yourself.

Feel excitement about everything the universe has to offer you—the gifts are endless. By respecting yourself and moving forward on your path, you'll see you've accessed a view which shows you how much more there is to be, do, know, learn, explore, enjoy, and love.

Respect everything and everyone, including, first and foremost, yourself. To do otherwise breaks your connection with the creative force which waits upon your self-love and your openness to show you your path, your purpose, and your intention.

We have two potential bug-a-boos when engaging our purpose. One is lack of self-love, and the other is a driving, occasionally strident, need to be right. Although these two "forces" may seem to be at odds with one another, they are often found in close proximity.

Lay Claim to Your Personal Strength

> *"You have power over your mind. Realize this, and you will find strength."*
> *Marcus Aurelius*

We can live our lives in a weakened, compromised position, or we can begin to shift our thoughts and actions to a position of strength.

In fact, everything in **Finding Your Path, Engaging Your Purpose** is about nurturing your autonomy and your unique strengths, weaving it all into one, meaningful, united STRENGTH.

Let's look at an issue that can—and does—erode a person's overall strength. This is the *need to be right*. We all have a *need to be right* to a greater or lesser degree.

Furthermore, it makes sense that we are generally right. If we were usually wrong, we most likely wouldn't still be here. It's a deep-seated part of our survival mechanism that dictates we *must be right*.

But because it's deep-seated, it's not particularly easy to access. And there is a definite downside to the need to be right.

> *"To make a mistake is only an error in judgment,*
> *But to adhere to it when it is discovered*
> *Shows infirmity of character."*
> **Dale E. Turner**

Consider—with the goal of shifting to strength—a question that Wayne Dyer so wisely posed:

"Do I have to be right
Or would I rather be happy?"

Being right and being happy are not always mutually exclusive, but, on another hand, *they often are*. How many friendships, parent-child relationships, marriages, border squabbles between countries, and horrifying international wars start over the striving insistence of being right rather than working toward being happy? A sign of maturity—for an individual, a family, a nation, a planet—is the ability to relinquish an inflexible stance.

We don't have to win every round, especially when "winning" has potential for loss. Meanwhile, happiness offers so much to gain.

Imagine raising your energy. What if every time you found yourself about to set your heels in and insist on being right, you consciously shift to being strong, focused, flexible and happy? As you shift to strength, imagine a powerhouse of happiness emanating from you. Forcing one's will upon others is not a powerful position. Role-modeling the behavior and *giving* the responses you'd like to *receive* is how to shift to strength. It will make you happy. It will make others happy.

The Challenge: Poor Self-Esteem

> *"We are each gifted in a unique*
> *And important way.*
> *It is our privilege and*
> *Our adventure to discover*
> *Our own special light."*
> **Mary Dunbar**

One of the attributes of poor self-esteem is the impression that one's world is out of control, and when the world feels out of control, there's a drive to control it.

This sense of out-of-control careening is often externalized and projected onto people and events, as the person experiencing poor self-esteem makes damaged efforts to feel in control. However, what is inside will not change by pushing at things that are outside.

Pushing on people and events can only lead to unpleasant or even disastrous results. What happens then? The undesirable results boomerang, feeding the monster of poor self-esteem ("I have no power") and control-freak energy ("I must increase my efforts to control").

Then others become dysfunctional as they attempt to jump through the shifting, flaming hoops of a control-freak's demands. Often they move away from this energy to protect themselves and manifest their own life.

An erroneous notion about your being—which, again, has been perfectly manifested—can well up from the subconscious in many unpleasant ways. This is the expression of "doing" from a damaged sense of "being."

Now is the time to choose to know that you are a perfect being. When about to enter an argument, or to direct someone's behavior, or to attempt to control some aspect of your universe, or *whenever* things seem out of control, ask yourself the following:

1. Do I want to be filled with discord, or would I prefer peace?

2. Do I prefer to be driven by anxiety, or would I prefer to be floating within joy?

3. Do I have to be "right" (even if I'm incorrect) or can I release the whole argument and quietly choose happiness?

4. Am I motivated by fear, which often expresses as anger, or am I motivated by unconditional love?

Focus on *your* path, *your* purpose. Each one of us is on our own journey. You can contribute to the highest outcome by engaging your *power of intention*.

> *"Self esteem is the reputation
> We acquire with ourselves."*
> **Nathaniel Branden**

Your Part

What is your definition of "self respect"?
_____
_____
_____
_____
_____
_____
_____
_____

What are three ways in which you can improve your self respect?

1._____
_____
_____
_____
_____
_____
_____
_____

2._____
_____
_____
_____
_____
_____
_____
_____

3. _____
_____
_____
_____
_____
_____

What is an insight you've had considering the question: Do I have to be right, or do I want to be happy?

_____
_____
_____
_____
_____
_____

What is one process or habit you can begin to change that is a *shift to strength*, wherein you will relinquish having to be right in preference to being happy?

_____
_____
_____
_____
_____
_____

Think about the relationship between self-respect and self-esteem. Write about the role each has within you. How can you improve this dynamic duo?

_____
_____
_____
_____
_____
_____
_____
_____

"Nothing is impossible.
*The word itself says **'I'm possible.'**"*
Audrey Hepburn

Chapter 9:

Adjust Your Perception
&
Pay Attention to Your Self-Talk

Adjust Your Perception

Have you ever noticed that the way you perceive an event is directly related to the emotions you experience? We've all heard someone—including ourselves—say, "You make me angry!"

But of course, no one can *make* you angry. Among the cast of characters known as our emotions, you choose which emotion to experience. Since anger is a disempowering emotion, why not choose curiosity, equanimity, or even choose to feel amused?

> *"You will not be punished **for** your anger*
> *You will be punished **by** your anger."*
> **Siddhārtha Gautama**

Consider this: you can adjust your perception about any situation, which will affect the pool of emotions you're likely to choose from. In other words, adjust your perception and what you perceive changes.

The way to lend power to this practice is to realize that first there is a thought and then—granted, with the faster-than-lightning speed of synapses—you choose an emotion. To allow your emotions to run riot within you is to allow the servant to become master, or to let a robot make programming decisions.

Become aware of that lightning quick moment between perceiving a data stream of information, and your emotional "reply." Here are some ways to begin to shift the habit of allowing emotions to have free rein in your life, to choosing the emotion that will give you more equanimity and personal power:

1. Make certain that your emotional reply is a *response*, not a *reaction*.

2. Consciously pause and choose a positive or neutral emotion to experience rather than choosing a negative or disempowering one.

3. Occasionally events are out of our control. Learn to let these events go. Choosing anger, hate, fear, victimization, self-pity and the like will not have any positive influence on the external events, while, at the same time, negative, reactive emotions take a huge toll on you.

• The more you adjust your perception and choose a positive or neutral emotion to experience, the more peaceful you'll be.

• The more peaceful you are, the more personal empowerment you'll experience.

• The more personal empowerment you experience, the greater your positive self-esteem.

• The more positive your self-esteem, the more you'll attract positive events and positive people to you.

Like attracts like. By changing your perceptions, you start a chain of events that bring happy-inducing events rather than sadness, or disempowering, or fear, or anger inducing experiences.

Pay Attention to Your Self-Talk

Paying attention to your internal dialogue is an important discipline when moving toward fulfilling your goals. Once again, the more fully you realize that what you think about expands and becomes manifest in the physical world, the more you'll become attuned to listening to your self-talk, and consciously bring it in line with your intentions, desires, and goals.

Take time to become conscious of all abusive, counter-productive, negative self-talk, and make a habit of reframing and rephrasing each incident until you've changed these habits, which are impediments to the road of self-manifestation.

Reframe

Rephrase

Affirm

Recapping from Chapter 7, "reframing" is the process of hearing and attending to negative, disempowering self-talk and rewriting or rephrasing it to become positive. From that rephrased statement, you develop an affirmation that may be widely applicable in your daily life.

You are a creator
You are creating your life
Listen to your self-talk
Choose your emotions
Change your perceptions
Your path becomes clear
As you engage your purpose

The Challenge: Jealousy & Envy

Jealousy

> *"Nor was jealousy understood...."*
> **John Milton**

The root word of jealousy is "zeal." People are certainly capable of being zealous when jealous!

But first, let's acknowledge that jealousy is as viable an emotion as any other. It has its reasons for being. Treating jealousy with appropriate attention and exploring the messages it's trying to communicate while reinforcing the growth potential it provides, is the best way to have an understanding of jealousy, and its less aggressive cousin, envy.

Jealousy—and envy—are emotions just as happiness, joy, fear, sadness, anger, excitement, and so forth, are emotions. One cannot successfully clamp the lid on any of them. You might feel like you're succeeding in hiding your jealousy, but, along with people saying things like, "he's more tightly wrapped than an egg roll," behind your back, you don't fool anyone but yourself. And you don't fool you either when the attempted suppression comes out in various ways such as anger and/or depression, and physical and psychological ills.

Jealousy arises from the basic drive for survival of the fittest. The gene pool urges individuals of any species to assure that *their* genetics are the ones contributing to future generations. The best way to assure *that* is to beat the competition, or to fluff up one's feathers to appear more attractive than the competition.

If an individual comes along who is strong, wily, clever, or beautiful enough to steal away the prime contributor(s) to future generations, those left behind will step up their efforts to recapture their mates or acquire new ones. Jealousy drives this mechanism, whether among humans or other creatures.

Interestingly, however, among humans, it seems, no emotion is held in such ill-repute as jealousy. Even anger is more allowable than jealousy. We're told we have a right to our anger, as long as we learn to express it responsibly. But this responsible attitude and tolerance is not permitted regarding jealousy. By and large the universal message about jealousy is that it's *WRONG, DON'T FEEL IT,* and if you do, *GET OVER IT.*

Envy

Jealousy is a fear that what one has may be taken away or who one is with may leave. Envy, on another hand, is a desire to have what someone else possesses. One doesn't necessarily want the same object (or person) that someone else has, you just want your own like it.

For example, let's say a friend has just bought a car you've dreamed of owning. But you're not happy for your friend. You're envious. It's not that you want *his* car, you want your own, and you're not the least bit pleased that you have to look at him having the car you long for.

A lot of people spend a lot of time contemplating and plotting how they can get an object, or relationship, like someone else has, allowing themselves to be miserable all the while.

Internal Dialogues

Both jealousy and envy have unpleasant internal dialogue scripts. It's not fun for the internal "you" to have to listen to them. These scripts create a lot of pain and don't provide any solutions.

Your Part:

Recall two self-talk incidents when you were jealous or envious and Reframe, Rephrase, and Affirm them:

1._____
_____
_____
_____

Reframe:_____
_____
_____
_____

Rephrase:_____
_____
_____
_____

Affirm:_____
_____
_____
_____

2._____
_____
_____
_____

Reframe:_____
_____
_____

Rephrase:_____
_____
_____

Affirm:_____
_____
_____

Chapter 10:
Kindness, Patience & Knowledge

> *"My religion is very simple.*
> *My religion is kindness."*
> **Dalai Lama**

Kindness & Patience

Kindness and patience are two primary and immutable forces of the creative universe. Patience is the state of Being from which boundless acts of inspiration flow and grow, while the emotion of kindness produces in our Doing state, acts of kindness. Patience is the bedrock underneath and the intelligence behind the emotion and the actions of kindness.

Practicing infinite patience and infinite kindness will bring you into a state of knowing that you're in harmony with the all-pervasive Creative force, and that you are in attunement with your individual, uniquely creative and manifesting energies.

> *"The greatest power is often simple patience."*
> E. Joseph Cossman

Kindness and patience are boomerangs! They will return to you. Have you ever had an occasion when you felt impatient and things rapidly fell apart, but when you became calm and patient and kind, everything fell into place?

I did! Just a few days ago. Pulling into the gas station, I was happy to see I didn't have to wait in line. I went into the little building to pay, as I was paying with cash.

I told the young attendant which pump I was at, then walked around my car to the pump, which was when I saw the small sign I couldn't see before, taped to the gas pump handle that there was only diesel available at this pump. Trekking back to the building, I noticed that in that couple of minutes, lines had formed at every row of pumps. I saw I'd have a hard time getting to any other pump.

I began to feel impatient.

Back inside the building, I had to stand in line. When I got the to front, I said to the teen-aged attendant, "You didn't tell me there's only diesel at the pump I'm at."

"Oh, I'm sorry," he answered, "I'll let you use the pump on the other side."

"All right." I gestured out the window, "but there's a line at all the pumps now, and I won't be able to negotiate getting to that pump without making people angry, because it'll look like I'm cutting in. Please come out with me to direct traffic."

"Okay," he answered.

I went back out, but he didn't come out, and sure enough, although I attempted to position my car at the other pump, and was clearly waiting for that pump, a gigantic truck from the other direction roared into my spot as soon as the car that was there pulled out. I trekked back for the third time to the little building, feeling really impatient. I had to stand in line again. When I got to the front I said, "I needed you to come out, and you didn't, and now that truck has come into my space, and is pumping gas on my forty dollars."

At this point, the attendant's boss got involved. They both went out to direct traffic, made cars pull back and forth to allow me in, everyone disgruntled. I ended up sitting behind a truck with a recreational boat in tow that took a considerable while to fill up.

But as I sat waiting, I reflected on "what just happened here?" Replaying how delighted I'd been that there initially was no line, yet all the ways this homely little situation became ever more complicated, I was left to contemplate the flow of energy, and also to contemplate what would be a meaningful response for me to the situation.

This meditation I'd just read in the morning by Jesse Jennings came to mind:

> "If something crosses your field of vision, then it has some business with you. You can ask the incoming information what it wants from you—it is sure to tell you and not be coy about it."

So the response to my, "What's up with this?" was an immediate, "*PATIENCE. KINDNESS.*"

Yes. I had become impatient. I had been less than kind. I had been stern with the high school attendant, no doubt new at the job. The situation clearly flustered him. I tried to defend my feelings by mentally arguing that my back hurt and I was late. What was the response from the universe?

"NO EXCUSES."

So I asked myself, "how would I like to be treated if the situation were reversed?"

By the time I pulled up to the pump, I had shifted to patience and kindness.

What was the result?

The manager kindly pumped my gas for me! We chatted and chuckled. I went back inside for my change, where the kid was braced for my disapproving attitude.

I said, "That was a fun adventure! I think I have some change."

He smiled, clearly relieved. "*That* part I can do."

We laughed. The energy completely shifted.

The manager came back inside. I said, "Thank you both so much!" They apologized. I said, "No problem!"

We wished one another a nice day and meant it.

Do we have to butt our heads against walls in order to practice kindness and patience?

Sometimes, apparently, yes. But it's easier, faster, and nicer if we don't.

> *"Kindness is the language*
> *Which the deaf can hear*
> *And the blind can see."*
> **Unknown**

Being infinitely kind to yourself as well as others will put you on your path and connect you to your purpose. Kindness is an essential feature of your attention to yourself—no matter what you're doing. Whether working, playing, being with family or friends, when alone, while working on changing habits, moving forward with personal growth, while relaxing—in short, in all of your thinking and feeling—always have your "prime directive" be that you intend kindness for yourself. Starting from your center, it will flow out to others.

Knowledge

> *"The larger the island of knowledge,*
> *The longer the shoreline of wonder."*
> **Ralph W. Sockman**

However you prefer to "name" the universal creative force—Mother-Father God, Creator, sentient energy, she-he, it, they—it has/they have "intended" you. As you've intentionally come into being, if you link up with this intentional knowing, you can see that your visions, dreams, ideas/ideals, goals, wishes, hopes and desires are no accident. You are motivated by the quiet urging of your potential by your Higher Self—engaged in human spiritual evolution with the Creator/Creative Force. We have been created to create.

The sooner you're about your business, your purpose, engaging and developing your skills, talents, creations, manifestations, and knowledge, the sooner the entire human family can progress, advancing to a higher understanding of creative being.

"A little knowledge that acts
Is worth infinitely more
Than much knowledge that is idle."

Khalil Gibran

Why are we on a trajectory of exponential scientific understanding wherein we've accrued more knowledge since WWII than all our previous time on the planet?

We are driven by some desire, some intention, inspired by the clockwork of some force, to ceaselessly peer into those clockworks and wonder about the workings of their mechanism.

Crows, horses, pythons, dogs, lions, crickets, trees, sunflowers, whales—so on and so on and so on—do not peer into the cosmic clockworks and wonder about their workings on a quest for knowledge. This fact does not make us superior, it just makes us have a reasoning curiosity that, even if we don't comprehend the why or wherefore of it at present, we must honor it with our focus of intention, with infinite patience.

> *"The beginning of knowledge*
> *Is the discovery of something*
> *We do not understand."*
> **Frank Herbert**

As we patiently—yet energetically!—accrue "knowledge," what has accompanied this knowledge? The answer is found in the most profound acts of kindness by millions and millions of people, acting in concert, as our little planet, Earth, has ever seen. In the wake of the Japanese tsunami and earthquake on March 11, 2011, hurricane Katrina, August 23 to August 30, 2005, the Indian Ocean Tsunami that ushered 2004 out the day after Christmas, and currently amidst our world-wide pandemic, the greatest mobilizations in history of aid, caring, and kindness have manifested.

Our instinct to be kind—because we are all kindred—rises to the surface.

> *"New knowledge is the most*
> *Valuable commodity on earth.*
> *The more truth we have to work with,*
> *the richer we become."*
> **Kurt Vonnegut**

Our potential to continually increase knowledge: of one another, of science, of the unknown, beckons us to study hard! Study your life, accrue your unique knowledge through whatever takes your fancy, occupies your mind, inhabits your dreams.

Knowledge is the root-system of the human family—be sure yours has grown deep, are well-watered and cultivated.

> *"If you have knowledge,*
> *Let others light their candles in it."*
> **Margaret Fuller**

The Challenge:
Practicing Relentless Forgiveness

What is it to practice relentless forgiveness? I've worked with many people who have a resistance against the very thought or sound of the words. There's an idea that forgiveness is a position of weakness, that to forgive someone gives them permission to continue.

But the opposite is the truth. Forgiveness is a process of pulling the plug on the attachment the abuser has to you. Holding onto the abuse by not forgiving is how one *becomes* a victim and *continues to be* a victim.

Inside the mind there is little difference between an event and the thought of an event. If someone has hurt or harmed you and it goes around and around in your mind, "this person hurt me, this person hurt me," every time you have that thought, to the mind it is as if it is real and the initial hurt is being re-enacted, again and again.

Furthermore, as many wisdom thinkers have said:

"Thoughts Become Things"

If thoughts become things, then every time you think, "that person harmed me," that thought is calling to become a physical reality. It calls for more harm, more hurt.

How do you break the chain? By practicing relentless forgiveness. Instead of going around and around with thoughts attached to the notion of being harmed, doesn't it seem wise to have thoughts that go around on the notion, the idea, the picture, of severing your tie with the energy of being harmed? Forgiveness is the knife that cuts through the cords that attach you to abuse.

Relentless forgiveness moves you from a position of being disempowered, fearful, hurt and angry, to one of releasing. So, by practicing forgiveness, you release the hold of that which is forgiven and everything attached to it. Fully engaged, relentless forgiveness is self-caring.

Forgiveness wipes that slate clean.

Getting into the habit of relentless, ongoing forgiveness may be a challenge at first, but the more you do it, the more it becomes a natural habit. You will discover amazing power in the practice of relentless forgiveness.

*"It's one of the greatest gifts you can give yourself,
To forgive. Forgive everybody."*
Maya Angelou

If you need a jumping-off point, here's an example of the conversation you might have with yourself:"(Name the person who has caused you harm) has hurt me in the past. I forgive you completely. I hereby sever the tie between us through which this hurt or harm flows. As long as you remain in my life, I will continue to practice relentless forgiveness, and I will continue to keep the channel through which you have previously hurt me severed.

"I forgive your lack of understanding regarding how your actions and words are hurtful. At the same time, I know that what we send out is what returns. I affirm that tolerance, peace, kindness and understanding are what return to me."

Your Part:
Kindness & Patience

Quietly contemplate your life. What are three situations that you can improve and heal by being kind and patient?

About each situation, first ask yourself, what about the situation makes you feel impatient?

Second, write a statement detailing how you can show your feelings of kindness through your behavior.

Third, make an affirmation about what the outcome will be.

Situation #1:

What is the situation, and how does it make me feel impatient?

_____
_____
_____
_____

How can I express my feelings of kindness by my behavior?

_____
_____
_____
_____

The positive outcome I envision by my shift to kindness and patience is:

_____
_____
_____
_____

Situation #2:

What is the situation, and how does it make me feel impatient?

_____
_____
_____
_____

How can I express my feelings of kindness by my behavior?

_____
_____
_____
_____

The positive outcome I envision by my shift to kindness and patience is:

_____
_____
_____
_____

Situation #3:

What is the situation, and how does it make me feel impatient?

_____
_____
_____
_____

How can I express my feelings of kindness by my behavior?

_____
_____
_____
_____

The positive outcome I envision by my shift to kindness and patience is:

_____
_____
_____
_____

Knowledge

Continuing in the vein of quiet introspection, what is a field of knowledge you've wanted to explore, but have not? The more we know, the more we grow. Adding to the storehouse of human knowledge adds to its wealth of compassion, health and abundance for everyone.

Honor your curiosity, increase your knowledge, improve life for yourself and others. Write down one big subject you've wanted to investigate and two smaller ones:

The big subject I would love to learn more about is:

_____
_____
_____
_____

A smaller subject I've been interested in is:

_____
_____
_____

Another smaller subject I've been interested in is:

_____
_____
_____
_____

Exciting! Why not begin your study today?

Chapter 11:
Kismet & Creation
&
Be What You Seek

Kismet and Creation

> *"Kismet: When you*
> *And the nature of the Universe*
> *Agree."*
> **Kismet Cowork**

Learn to listen to your thoughts and and to hear your intuition. Sometimes it may seem that a thought is very small and insignificant, and yet it is so "niggle-y," it keeps returning. Sometimes it even seems as though the external world is in cahoots with this thought. An ad, a headline, a phrase on TV, in a movie ... echoes, somehow, a thought or feeling you've been noticing—or, perhaps, ignoring.

Don't ignore it. These thoughts and/or feelings are messages from your intuition. You will learn to listen to these "coincidences," and discover that they are intentional. When you dare to affirm that there are no accidents, your life becomes exponentially driven by your intention, and "coincidences" happen regularly.

You'll sometimes be amazed, and even amused, by the endless kismet, serendipity, in your life. Knowledge will come to you in a flash. You'll be at the right place at the right time. Opportunities will manifest that are exactly what is needed at that moment for the purpose of engaging your purpose, *if you have clarity of vision.*

Make a clear picture of your heart's desire for your purpose, then release this picture. You don't have to know everything, right now, about how to be within your purpose. You only need to know your heart's desire and *believe in the vision.* When you get there, there you'll be!

*"There is no greater joy
than that of feeling oneself a creator.
The triumph of life
is expressed by creation."*
Henri Bergson

The powers of attraction are profound immutable laws of the seen and unseen universe. As Dr. Wayne Dyer wrote in his book **Real Magic**, science has come to realize that the previously supposed "nothingness" between any and all the "somethings" (a chair, a proton, a planet) is a web of sentience. A knowing something-ness.

Previously, the stance of science has been that everything that is, comes from something else that already is. But now quantum physics is postulating that (as spiritual Masters have said throughout time) "stuff" manifests, apparently, from nothing.

From the synapses of your brain, where you imagine in you mind (which is both the physical matter that resides inside your head, as well as "mind energy" that is hooked up to the larger web of *MIND* external to physical matter) that which has never been before. A work of art, a human relationship, a spiritual illumination, a healing, a kindness, an invention—*whatever* your mind imagines, your brain synapses.

These synapses put manifestation (creation) into motion. Lightning and chemistry on the planet stimulated life, and "lightning" (electrical synapse) and chemistry in your brain also stimulate life, i.e., creation.

> *"The whole difference between*
> *Construction and creation*
> *Is exactly this: a thing constructed*
> *Can only be loved after it is constructed*
> *But a thing created is loved before it exists."*
> **Charles Dickens**

Guard your thoughts! As you move forward on your path and engage your purpose, you will shorten the time and the distance between a thought and its manifestation. That's why it's important to have thoughtful and intentionally worded affirmations—keep your language positive, keep your path uncluttered, keep your intention focused, and engage your purpose with joy, peace and happiness.

> *"Every human is an artist.*
> *And this is the main art that we have:*
> *The creation of our story."*
> **Don Miguel Ruiz**

Be What You Seek

> *"The golden opportunity you are seeking*
> *Is within yourself."*
> **Orison Sweet Marden**

Be what you seek, ever mindful and conscious of your being. Because you are indeed drawing to you events, things, and people that are the manifestation of the lightning synapses you are setting off in your brain.

You are amazingly unique. There is something in your presence, talents, skills, knowing, being, and doing that you can use to advance yourself, which also advances the entire human family.

You have free will. You can also choose not to do your growth, not to fulfill your talents. Perhaps that's been your choice—until now.

BE (think/feel) and DO (act) kind, confident, generous, trusting, strong, intelligent, talented, skilled and loving, and this is what will return to you in response to your "ad." That is to say, the request sent out by your synapses that contains your beliefs, intentions and heart's desire will give you what you request.

> *"Dare to break through barriers*
> *To find your own path."*
> **Les Brown**

Your beliefs, intentions, and heart's desire need to be focused. If diffuse or negative energy is manifesting in your life, you will need to discover where the leakage is. Where are you harboring disbelief, diffused purpose, or cross-purpose intentions?

For instance, if you have an intention to learn to knit, but you cannot release the energy around your mother saying that she simply never had the patience or skill to learn to knit, and you choose to "own" her self-limiting paradigm for yourself also, you'll be at cross-purposes. The tricky part is when your mother's paradigm is in your subconscious and you don't consciously know that you hold this picture.

So be clear about what you seek. If what manifests is at cross-purposes or counter productive, you can ask your Id, Ego, and Higher Self to discover what is impeding you.

You absolutely can do this on your own, while it can also be helpful to have someone else track what comes up for you when you're doing this work. It can be a friend who is also on a higher path—although at times finding such a friend can be more rare than hen's teeth. You might also work with a counselor who focuses on both psychological and spiritual paths, who will help you keep your focus on manifesting your intentions and your purpose.

"What you seek is seeking you."
Rumi

Also, please keep in mind that sometimes a pile-up of negative-seeming events occur in order to rapidly clear your path. Be patient when things appear to be going wrong in every direction. *BE PATIENT*. Allow time and space to move out the muddle and you may see that all the unpleasantness was precisely what needed to happen to assist you in moving forward.

*"Nature ... has no effect without cause
Nor invention without necessity."*
Leonardo da Vinci

The Challenge: Understanding Cause–Effect

> *"Strong people believe in cause and effect."*
> Ralph Waldo Emerson

Results are at Effect

In order to change results, you must attend to cause. Your behavior is at cause. Behavior–cause needs to change in order for results–effect to change. Sometimes a cause was set in motion a long time ago, before you knew what you are now learning, and the effect of that cause must be worked through. However, now you can clear that negative cause-effect chain without setting the same cause in motion again.

There is a learning curve involved in understanding how we put an *effect* into motion by our own at cause behaviors. We often don't see this relationship and we miss the mechanics of how it works. Let's look at an example.

I have, unhappily, worked with entirely too many people who have been physically and/or psychologically abused by their significant other. These relationships are complicated and almost always have layers of cause-effect, cause-effect. But, stripping it down to the simplest consideration, what I would like anyone in this situation to realize is that "being abused" is at "effect." At "cause" is the behavior, the choice, of staying where one is abused.

I've heard every defensive argument ever contrived around this dynamic, most of which begins, "I can't afford..." and if that's the affirmation a person needs to make, no one can change that person's mind or affirmation. But many, many people *do* decide to change their affirmations *and* their lives for the better.

It is possible.

Being abused is a cause-effect relationship. Staying with an abuser is a choice to behave in the same manner—which is the "cause" with an expectation of a different result, which is the "effect." But the same cause will produce the same effect. Believing otherwise is not true, not healthy, and, candidly, not the best application of one's intelligence.

As stated elsewhere, continuing to do the same thing with the expectation of a different result is a definition of insanity.

The more you honestly *consider* your actions at cause, the more you will *change* your actions at cause. Thus, the more the effects—your life experiences—will be in alignment with your heart's desires.

Your Part:

What is something—either recently or in the past—that you feel was at cross-purposes with your affirmations or intentions?

Sit quietly and ask your mind to present an awareness or a picture of what you allowed to cause the cross-purpose.

When it comes up, write it out spontaneously. Don't concern yourself with form, spelling, legibility, appearance or even logical sense. Just write until you're through writing. If it's a picture, sketch it, if it's both, draw and write, write and draw.

Do not be judgmental of anything that comes up, just allow it to shoulder its way through thoughts, feelings, walls, gates, criticism, surprise, fear, anger, or any other such emotion, mechanism or road block. It is probable that if something has dived subliminally into denial, there will be a wall and/or gate keeper.

_____
_____
_____
_____
_____
_____
_____

When you are done with the spontaneous writing, write a list of the emotions you are now aware of that you felt while writing.

I've noticed, somewhat surprisingly, that many people have a hard time thinking of the names of emotions. So here's a short list of a few that are likely to come up while you are looking at events or circumstances that were at cross-purposes with your affirmations and intentions:

anxiety / fear / anger / lost / hate / depression / screaming-meemies / guilt / pity / hysteria / unloved / relief / calm / insight / epiphany / "a-ha!" / joy / peace / happiness / and / or a sense of integration. That feeling of integration is not exactly, of itself, an emotion, but the experience of several healthy emotions, coming together with clarifying thoughts.

List of emotions that came up while writing what was at cross-purposes with my affirmations and intentions:

_____
_____
_____
_____
_____
_____

Be What You Seek — What You Seek is Present

Chapter 12:

Gratitude, Love, & Wisdom

*"Gratitude is a twofold love —
Love coming to visit us, and love
Running out to greet a welcome guest."*
Henry Van Dyke

Gratitude

We have come full circle in the exploration of Finding Your Path, Engaging Your Purpose—and yet not exactly. The Path to Purpose is an ever-climbing spiral. If you find yourself thinking, "I've been here before," pause and take inventory of the arduous and inspired upward journey you've undertaken that brings you to a familiar, yet expanded, view, an expanded awareness.

Where are you now, what experiences have you had, what lessons have you learned, what feelings have you experienced, that were not a part of you the previous time you arrived at this location?

Life Lessons

> *"In daily life we must see that*
> *It is not happiness that makes us grateful,*
> *But gratitude that makes us happy."*
> **Brother David Steindl-Rast**

In my private psychotherapy practice I observed that every individual has a particular set of "Lessons to Learn," if one chooses to learn them. But we can choose, in this lifetime, not to do the work that comes to us. We can choose not to learn the lessons, not to get on the path, not to engage in our unique purpose.

By "activating" the explorations in the twelve chapters of **Finding Your Path, Engaging Your Purpose**, you've embarked on your life's work, both external—what you *"DO,"* and internal— who you *"BE."* You've contemplated various considerations of how your psychological and spiritual self engages in life.

> *"Gratitude makes sense of our past*
> *Brings peace for today and*
> *Creates a vision for tomorrow."*
> **Melody Beattie**

Now, let's put emphasis on the process that moves your actions of growth, learning, and exploration, and your emotional states of joy, peace, and happiness, into warp drive. This process is *active gratitude*.

It's wonderful and amazing to live in a time and in place where you are able to live your life according to your Sense of Purpose.

Be grateful for your numerous freedoms. If this seems untrue for you, comb through your choices, and be honest regarding how choices you previously made may curtail the choices you now desire to make.

> *"The Universe loves Gratitude.*
> *The more Grateful you are,*
> *The more goodies you get."*
> **Louise Hay**

Be grateful *every day* for your physical senses—the ability to see, taste, touch, hear and smell. Don't forget to say thank you.

"Thank you for my ability to smell the frying onions, the loamy earth, thank you for my ability to taste the apple, the chai tea, thank you for the feeling of soft silk, the texture of a leaf, thank you for the sound of the lovely music, the geese flying overhead, or the near silence in which I hear a gentle breeze in the evergreens. Thank you for being able to see the ocean waves, the child's smile, the starlit night."

Be grateful for your mind that thinks and your emotions that feel. Be thankful for the Greater Something that grants you intuition, empathy, intention, intelligence, and your sense of purpose.

Be grateful for every one of your life experiences, whether you name it "good" or "bad." There is no "bad" when you are on your path, there are only lessons.

Be grateful for your path and your intention. Be grateful that you woke up to the urgency of doing that which expands your being.

> *"Gratitude is happiness Doubled by wonder."*
> **Gilbert K. Chesterton**

Love — The Greatest Truth

> *"I believe that the reason of life*
> *Is for each of us simply to grow in love."*
> **Leo Tolstoy**

As we come to a close, let us appreciate the greatest truth of all, which is to extend, to inspire, and to receive LOVE.

Extend love to all, even those who have harmed, hurt, or abused you, even to those who have been weak, selfish, or cruel. Love is stronger than all of these emotions and attributes put together.

Love is at the heart of all true, meaningful, effective, and motivating/motivational emotions. The closer to love a feeling, a motivation, an inspiration, the more powerful and productive it is.

> *"Happiness cannot be traveled to,*
> *Owned, earned, worn or consumed.*
> *Happiness is the spiritual experience*
> *Of living every minute with love, grace,*
> *And gratitude."*
> **Denis Waitley**

Extending authentic, energetic, uncontaminated love, i.e., metta, to those who have harmed or hurt you is the most infallible tool you have to render impotent whatever is feeding the source of hurt. You do not have to accept abuse in any form, under any circumstance. Once you are at a distance from abuse, it is possible to imagine loving thoughts sent to heal the situation and to heal the abuser.

Be Love, and in being love, you are on your path, you are engaging your purpose. No matter what the "doing" aspect of your path and purpose is, when you clearly and truthfully consider your goals, they well up from you being, which first and foremost, loves.

> *"Love is the only reality*
> *And it is not a mere sentiment.*
> *It is the ultimate truth*
> *That lies at the heart of creation."*
> **Rabindranath Tagore**

Wisdom

> *"The mind once enlightened*
> *Cannot again become dark."*
> **Thomas Paine**

Love loves wisdom. Love and wisdom are great friends, where insights are shared. Both are ever-present to help us and to companion us on Life's

Journey. There is nothing to fear and so much to enjoy when you are cloaked in love and open to receiving your wisdom.

It is possible gain wisdom—in addition to knowledge—from, for example, reading a book or listening to a lecture. But then, again you may not. Wisdom occurs when you stamp you own brand of insight-filled *"a-ha!"* onto information, life experiences, or knowledge.

Wisdom is where knowledge aspires to rest. Though your life may be filled with challenges, sadness, fear, grief, and anger—*and every life is!*—wisdom is standing by for you to find your solace and, well, *wisdom*.

> *"Knowledge comes*
> *But wisdom lingers."*
> **Alfred Lord Tennyson**

Perhaps a way to contemplate the acquisition of wisdom is to be childlike in your observations, and adult-like in claiming the meaning of your observations.

Wisdom's insights may come as you contemplate your ideas of right and wrong, or when you hold yourself accountable for your thoughts and deeds, or when you affirm it is wise to always be truthful. Through the acquisition of your wisdom virtues develop.

> *"Honesty is the first chapter in the book of wisdom."*
> ***Thomas Jefferson***

Wisdom teaches us about the human virtues of empathy, compassion, and kindness, as we become ever more self-aware of our emotions and thoughts. However you develop your wisdom, you will know it by its unshakable-yet-flexible nature. Like any healthy foundation, it stands strong, but can take an earthquake.

What Wisdom is Not

Wisdom is not putting your head in the sand—attempting to block information—when a challenging experience occurs, or when you read or see something that makes you uncomfortable, frightened, or angry.

Wisdom is not a *Big Book of Rules*. Shoulds and should nots are for those who are not able to discover their own wisdom and, instead, cite a particular *Big Book of Rules* as if it's their wisdom. Wisdom does not dictate. Wisdom waits quietly, sharing its insights when listened to, and remaining quiet when there is minimal chance of being heard.

> *"The desire to reach for the stars is ambitious.
> The desire to reach hearts is wise."*
> *Maya Angelou*

You will find solace and growth in your accruing wisdom when you treat it with honor and respect. What is especially lovely and meaningful about wisdom is that it gives you the space in which to process physical, psychological, and spiritual pain as you remove yourself from the debilitating aspects of uncertainty, jealousy, fear, and hate. In moving above these debilitating emotional reactions, you will be able to calmly *respond*.

> *"May Your Wounds become Wisdom."*
> *D. Simone*

Illusive Wisdom

If wisdom is still a mystery to you, contemplate your feelings of compassion, empathy, kindness, and unconditional love toward people, animals, plants, and the planet, and how you express these feelings.

Your wisdom encourages you to move from the confines of societal norms, religious constructs, and familial constraints, to the place where *WISDOM* resides. Within your citadel of wisdom you begin to truly comprehend the power, the beauty, and the meaning of nature and of life. You come closer to the Creative Force, in whwatever way you may name it.

> *"Knowing yourself*
> *Is the beginning of all wisdom."*
> ***Aristotle***

The Heart of Wisdom

In wisdom, you see the purpose of your life. Wisdom supports you in your efforts to be engaged in your purpose, even when it seems everyone else has turned away. Sometimes we need to have everyone turn away so we can see ourselves *through our own eyes*—not everyone else's.

> *"Yesterday I was clever,*
> *So I wanted to change the world.*
> *Today I am wise,*
> *So I am changing myself."*
> ***Rumi***

Your emotional and spiritual progress is possible by virtue of your wisdom. Wisdom knows what is just, what is true. Wisdom forgives.

Wisdom shines a brilliant, revealing light on greed, avarice, and superficial desires, showing us that *we are all in this together*. Wisdom provides us peace of mind through awakening our dormant higher consciousness, calming the mind of chaos, and providing an understanding of contentedly accepting life the way it is.

May your wisdom grow and blossom as you continue on your unique path, fulfilling your purpose.

The Challenge: Being at Peace With Everyone

"Peace is not something you wish for
It's something you make
Something you do
Something you are
And something you give away."
Robert Fulghum

Being at peace with everyone is a daily challenge. One does not say, "I am, from now on, going to be at peace with everyone," and it's done. No. One must reaffirm this challenge every day.

Being at peace with everyone means—being at peace with *everyone*.

It includes the technical service person on the other end of the phone, your business partner, your boss, your spouse, your mother, your father, your children, your best friend, your former best friend, the rude shop keeper, the self-involved teenager, the person who cut you off on the highway, the mortgage broker, the person with a different religion, the person with different politics, the person with a different cultural background, the person with a different color of skin, the crying baby on the airplane, the teacher, the preacher, the priest, the shaman, the radio host, the journalist, the heads of state, the terrorist.

EVERYONE.

Here's the advantage. Being at peace with everyone *makes peace*. Being at odds with and feeding negative energy toward anyone augments—that is to say, *feeds*—the very thing you despise.

> *"The first peace ...*
> *Is that which comes within the souls*
> *of people [who] realize their oneness*
> *with the universe and all its powers.*
> *When they realize*
> *at the center of the universe*
> *dwells the Great Spirit,*
> *and that its center is everywhere.*
> *It is within each of us."*
> **Black Elk**

Energy moves where you send it. As saying has it, "Energy flows where attention goes."

Energy is a *force* of the seen and the unseen world. It is incapable of making judgments. To energy, there is no "good" and no "bad" energy. It cannot have thoughts about itself. We are the makers of the notions of good and bad.

> *"You'll never find peace of mind*
> *Until you listen to your heart."*
> **George Michael**

We make the lightning bolts of energy. Your negative energy flows right to the source of what irritates or angers you, feeding the negative. Your anger is fuel (energy) to the fire (situation).

Think of a moment when you've been so angry that you could have "spit nails." Step back from that emotion, and the situation that provoked it. Contemplate the intensity of your energy. What if the energy you manifested was in physical form, right there in front of you? If you're successful in picturing your anger as physical, you may be astonished at what it looks like and the intensity of it.

Imagine this—multiply your vision of this anger times several billion, every single day, roiling around on our little planet.

Sometimes one just has to marvel that we're still here.

> *"For every minute you remain angry,*
> *You give up sixty seconds of peace."*
> ***Ralph Waldo Emerson***

But we *are still here*. We're still here, surely, in part, because there are knowing individuals performing metta in meditation, mindfully creating unconditional love, somewhere on the planet every minute of every day. There are love-centered people, praying for peace, mindfully creating unconditional love, somewhere on the planet every minute of every day.

And we are still here because people are owning their joy, peace, and happiness. The more you remove yourself from giving power to anger, frustration, negative thoughts, the more you mindfully create unconditional love, the more you will heal the negatives in your life.

The more you produce the energy of metta that you send to those who hurt, abuse, anger or oppress anyone, the more neutral their power to hurt, abuse, anger or oppress anyone becomes.

Through love all that is bitter will be sweet."
Jalaluddin Rumi

Move forward through your life with a clarity of purpose that nurtures peace, joy, and happiness. When you are inside peace radiating joy, this is a gift to everyone, including yourself.

"Peace begins with a smile. "
Mother Teresa

Your Part:

1. Picture someone you do not like and mindfully create neutral feelings with an intention of arriving at unconditional love. Reflect on your own power that you've given up in deciding not to like someone for a variety of reasons that, perhaps, have to do with your perception of how that person has hurt or harmed you.

Creating metta—unconditional love—for that person takes the hurt out of you and sends healing love to the other person. Generally speaking, people hurt others because they, themselves, are hurting. Maybe they show that hurt as anger, as abuse, as sarcasm, as power-mongering, as discrimination, as physical abuse.

Remove yourself from this negative environment and send unconditional love to their source of pain from your source of loving-kindness.

To be clear: this is not an approval of that person's psychological abuse, power-mongering, sociopathy, physical abuse, or any other negative behaviors and attitudes. This is a process of you removing yourself from these negative expressions of energy, and being able to, *by the power and energy of unconditional love.*

2. Write about three occasions over the last few weeks since you became committed to **Finding Your Path, Engaging Your Purpose** where you

experienced kindness—whether given or received—which may not have transpired before you embarked on this journey. And, yes, the subtle shifts in *yourself* may result in receiving kindness that you may not have in the past.

1. _____
_____
_____

2. _____
_____
_____

3. _____
_____
_____

3. Write about three occasions where you experienced love—whether given or received—which, again, may not have transpired before taking this journey.

1. _____
_____
_____

2. _____
_____
_____

3. _____
_____
_____

Nothing is Lost in the Mind of the Creator

In Closing

A Final Exercise

Let us revisit the *How Full is Your Glass* exercise. Compare your current results with the first time you did this exercise.

Are there some interesting changes in your life?

How Full Is Your Glass?

Put a mark on each glass, from empty to full, and write a number from 1 to 10 by the glass to indicate the amount of fulfillment you experience in your life regarding the named aspect.

Write the positive events, actions, thoughts and feelings in the glass below the line that fill the glass to that point, and write above the line anything that is not at present in the glass that would make it a "10," or that is preventing it from becoming a "10."

Example: I draw a line on Physical Health above the middle and write "7." Below the line I might write "yoga" and "good diet" as things that contribute to my health, and above the line I might indicate "knee injury" that affects my physical health.

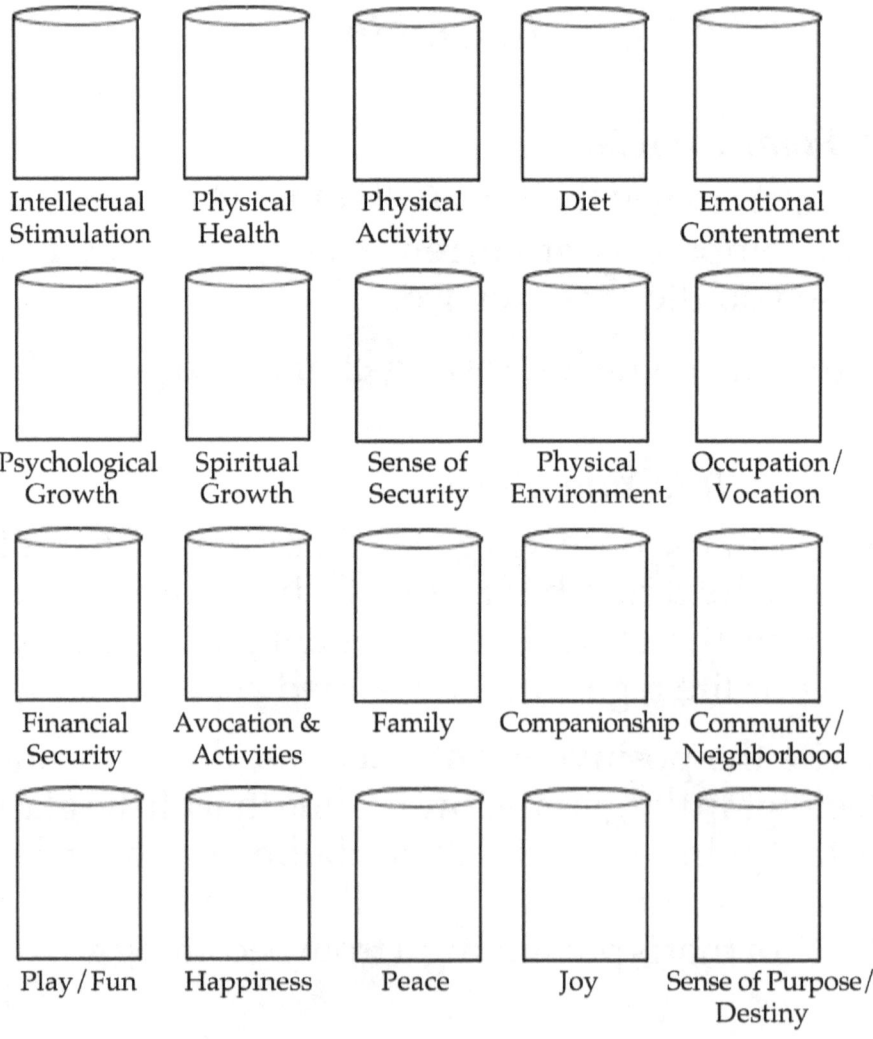

194 —— *Finding Your Path, Engaging Your Purpose*

Thank you for going on this journey with me. I pray for you all the wonderful joy and happiness that being engaged in your life's purpose will provide you. You are amazing! This was not an easy path, but life's greatest treasures are worth some effort, are they not? We each have a different path, but we all have the same goal—fulfilling our potential.

Never forget how unique and precious you are, intended with immeasurable *LOVE* by the Creator/Creative Force. Remember, the Bible affirms not once but twice, in both the Old Testament and the New Testament:

> *"Ye are gods."*
> **Psalms 82:6**
> **John 10:34**

My Gift for You....

Thank you for working your way through *Finding Your Path, Engaging Your Purpose*. I'd like to give you a gift of my ebook. ***Horn of Plenty – The Cornucopia of Your Life***. Type in the following URL to download your copy:

https://blytheayne.com/horn-of-plenty

About the Author....

I live in a forest with a few domestic and numerous wild creatures, where I create an ever-growing inventory of books, both nonfiction and fiction, short stories, illustrated kid's books, and articles, with a bit of wood carving when I need a change of pace.

I received my Doctorate from the University of California at Irvine in the School of Social Sciences, majoring in psychology and ethnography, after which I moved to the Pacific Northwest to write and to have a modest private psychotherapy practice in a small town not much bigger than a village. Finally I decided it was time to put my full focus on my writing, where, through the world-shrinking internet, I could "meet" greater numbers of people. *Where I could meet you!*

All the creatures in my forest and I are glad you "stopped by." If **Finding Your Path, Engaging Your Purpose** has touched you in a positive way, I hope you'll share it with others.

If you'd like to write me, I'm happy to hear from you:

Blythe@BlytheAyne.com

www.BlytheAyne.com

May you be happy, may you be well, may you be filled with joy!

Metta,
Blythe

REFERENCES:

Gregg Braden:
Turning Point
The Wisdom Codes: Ancient Words to Rewire Our Brains and Heal Our Hearts
The Divine Matrix: Bridging Time, Space, Miracles, and Belief
The Spontaneous Healing of Belief: Shattering the Paradigm of False Limits
The God Code
The Science of Self-Empowerment: Awakening the New Human Story
The Isaiah Effect: Decoding the Lost Science of Prayer and Prophecy
Secrets of the Lost Mode of Prayer: The Hidden Power of Beauty, Blessing, Wisdom, and Hurt
Resilience from the Heart: The Power to Thrive in Life's Extremes
Fractal Time: The Secret of 2012 and a New World Age
Deep Truth: Igniting the Memory of Our Origin, History, Destiny, and Fate
Entanglement (Tales of Everyday Magic)

Depak Chopra:
Metahuman: Unleashing Your Infinite Potential
The Seven Spiritual Laws of Success: A Practical Guide to the Fulfillment of Your Dreams
The Seven Spiritual Laws of Yoga: A Practical Guide to Healing Body, Mind, and Spirit
Total Meditation: Practices in Living the Awakened Life
You Are the Universe: Discovering Your Cosmic Self and Why It Matters
The Book of Secrets: Unlocking the Hidden Dimensions of Your Life
The Healing Self: A Revolutionary New Plan to Supercharge Your Immunity and Stay Well for Life
Creating Affluence: The A-to-Z Steps to a Richer Life
The Shadow Effect: Illuminating the Hidden Power of Your True Self
Super Brain: Unleashing the Explosive Power of Your Mind to Maximize Health, Happiness, and Spiritual Well-Being

Buddha: A Story of Enlightenment
Reinventing the Body, Resurrecting the Soul: How to Create a New You
The Spontaneous Fulfillment of Desire: Harnessing the Infinite Power of Coincidence
The Third Jesus: The Christ We Cannot Ignore
How to Know God: The Soul's Journey Into the Mystery of Mysteries
Super Genes: Unlock the Astonishing Power of Your DNA for Optimum Health and Well-Being
The Way of the Wizard: Twenty Spiritual Lessons for Creating the Life You Want
Jesus: A Story of Enlightenment
The Path to Love: Spiritual Strategies for Healing
Ageless Body, Timeless Mind: The Quantum Alternative to Growing Old
God: A Story of Revelation
Power, Freedom, and Grace: Living from the Source of Lasting Happiness
Finding Our True Home: Living in the Pure Land Here and Now
Transformation and Healing: The Four Foundations of Consciousness Sutra
And others

Louise Hay:
You Can Heal Your Life
Heal Your Body: The Mental Causes for Physical Illness and the Metaphysical Way to Overcome Them
The Power Is Within You
Trust Life: Love Yourself Every Day
All Is Well: Heal Your Body with Medicines, Affirmations, and Intuition
Loving Yourself to Great Health: Thoughts & Food
Gratitude: A Way of Life
Life Loves You: 7 Spiritual Practices to Heal Your Life
I Can Do It Affirmations: How to Use Affirmations to Change Your Life
You Can Create an Exceptional Life
Heart Thoughts: A Treasury of Inner Wisdom
Experience Your Good Now!: Learning to Use Affirmations
Life!: Reflections on Your Journey

The Times of Our Lives: Extraordinary True Stories of Synchronicity, Destiny, Meaning, and Purpose
101 Ways to Happiness
Modern-Day Miracles
Everyday Positive Thinking

The Dalai Lama:
The Book of Joy: Lasting Happiness in a Changing World
The Art of Happiness
An Introduction to Buddhism
An Open Heart: Practicing Compassion in Everyday Life
The Dalai Lama's Little Book of Wisdom
Approaching the Buddhist Path
The Universe in a Single Atom: The Convergence of Science and Spirituality
Beyond Religion: Ethics for a Whole World
How To Practice: The Way to a Meaningful Life
Our Only Home: A Climate Appeal to the World
How to See Yourself As You Really Are
Emotional Awareness: Overcoming the Obstacles to Psychological Balance and Compassion
The Four Noble Truths
Perfecting Patience: Buddhist Techniques to Overcome Anger
Essence of the Heart Sutra: The Dalai Lama's Heart of Wisdom Teachings
Buddhism: One Teacher, Many Traditions
Kindness, Clarity, and Insight: The Fundamentals of Buddhist Thought and Practice
The Complete Foundation: The Systematic Approach to Training the Mind
The Good Heart: A Buddhist Perspective on the Teachings of Jesus
A Profound Mind: Cultivating Wisdom in Everyday Life
Be Happy
And others

Bruce Lipton:
The Biology of Belief

The Honeymoon Effect: The Science of Creating Heaven on Earth
Spontaneous Evolution

Lynne McTaggart:
The Field: The Quest for the Secret Force of the Universe
The Power of Eight: Harnessing the Miraculous Energies of a Small Group to Heal Others, Your Life, and the World
The Intention Experiment: Using Your Thoughts to Change Your Life and the World
The Bond: How to Fix Your Falling-Down World
Heart Disease: Drug-Free Alternatives to Prevent and Reverse Heart Disease (What Doctors Don't Tell You)

Carolyn Myss:
Intimate Conversations with the Divine: Prayer, Guidance, and Grace
Anatomy of the Spirit: The Seven Stages of Power and Healing
Sacred Contracts: Awakening Your Divine Potential
Archetypes: A Beginner's Guide to Your Inner-net
Entering the Castle: An Inner Path to God and Your Soul
Why People Don't Heal and How They CanInvisible Acts of Power: The Divine Energy of a Giving Heart
Defy Gravity: Healing Beyond the Bounds of Reason
The Creation of Health: The Emotional, Psychological, and Spiritual Responses That Promote Health and Healing

Don Miguel Ruiz:
The Four Agreements: A Practical Guide to Personal Freedom
The Mastery of Love: A Practical Guide to the Art of Relationship
The Fifth Agreement: A Practical Guide to Self-Mastery
The Voice of Knowledge: A Practical Guide to Inner Peace
The Five Levels of Attachment: Toltec Wisdom for the Modern World
The Circle of Fire: Inspiration and Guided Meditations for Living in Love and Happiness
Wisdom of the Shamans: What the Ancient Masters Can Teach Us about Love and Life

The Three Questions: How to Discover and Master the Power Within You
The Mastery of Life: A Toltec Guide to Personal Freedom
Prayers: A communion with our Creator

Rumi:
The Book of Love: Poems of Ecstasy and Longing
The Essential Rumi (Coleman Barks, translator)The Book of Love: Poems of Ecstasy and Longing (Coleman Barks, translator)The Big Red Book: The Great Masterpiece Celebrating Mystical Love and Friendship (Coleman Barks, translator)A Year with Rumi: Daily Readings (Coleman Barks, translator)Michael Talbot:
The Holographic Universe
Mysticism and the New Physics
Your Past Lives – A Reincarnation
Beyond the Quantum
The Delicate Dependency

Eckhart Tolle:
The Power of Now: A Guide to Spiritual Enlightenment
A New Earth: Awakening to Your Life's Purpose
Stillness Speaks

Gary Zukav:
The Dancing Wu Li Masters: An Overview of the New Physics
The Seat of the Soul
Universal Human: Creating Authentic Power and the New Consciousness
Spiritual Partnership: The Journey to Authentic Power
Soul Stories
The Heart of the Soul: Emotional Awareness
The Mind of the Soul: Responsible Choice
Soul to Soul: Communications from the Heart

www.ingramcontent.com/pod-product-compliance
Lightning Source LLC
Chambersburg PA
CBHW030324100526
44592CB00010B/560